The Buildings
of Winchester

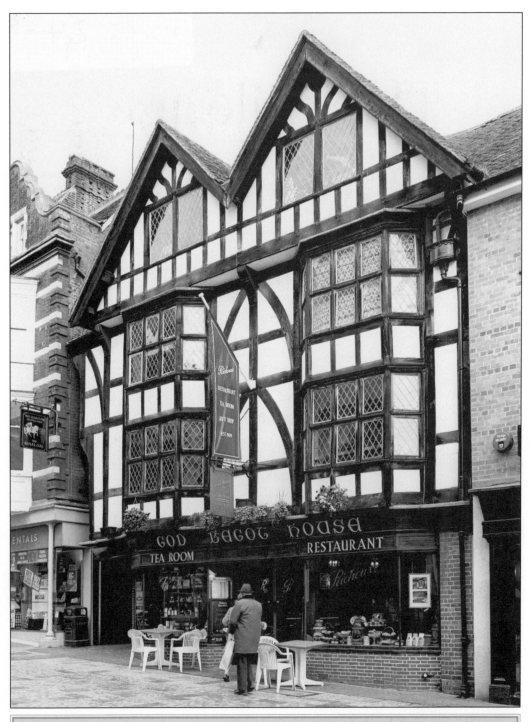

1 The High Street façade of Godbegot House is only a nineteenth-century facsimile of the real sixteenth-century framing – but impressive nevertheless. This was one half of a longer façade to a whole block of tenements and shops, much of which survives.

The Buildings of Winchester

RICHARD K. MORRISS

With photographs by Ken Hoverd

ALAN SUTTON PUBLISHING LIMITED

First published in the United Kingdom in 1994
Alan Sutton Publishing Limited
Phoenix Mill · Far Thrupp · Stroud · Gloucestershire

First published in the United States of America in 1994
Alan Sutton Publishing Inc. · 83 Washington Street · Dover
NH 03820

British Library Cataloguing in Publication Data

A catalogue record for this book is available from the British
Library.

ISBN 0–7509–0564–6

Library of Congress Cataloging in Publication Data applied for

Cover illustrations: front: *the Butter Cross in the High Street*;
inset: *the medieval West Gate*; back: *detail of the guildhall.*

Typeset in 11/14 Times.
Typesetting and origination by
Alan Sutton Publishing Limited.
Printed in Great Britain by
Ebenezer Baylis, Worcester.

Contents

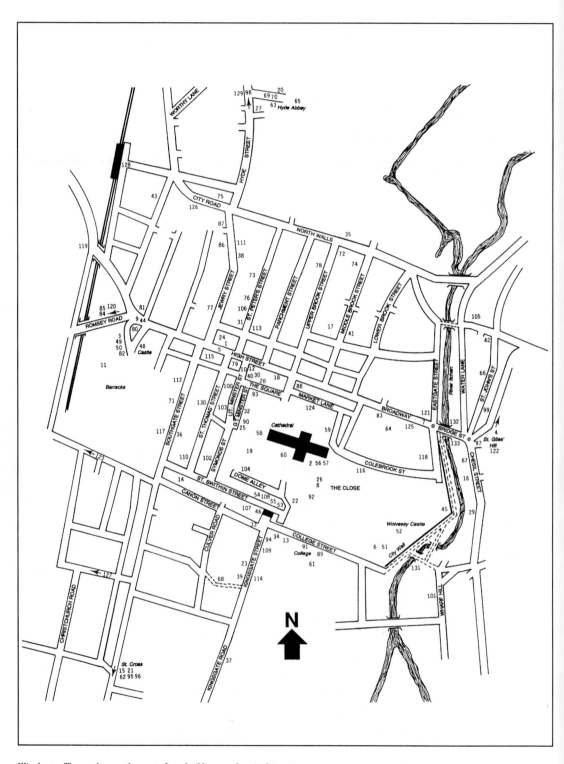

Winchester. The numbers on the map refer to building numbers in the captions.

Introduction

*Winchester is a large town [that] was once the metropolis;
there is a wall encompassing it with severall Gates, the
streets are pretty good large and long, the buildings but low
and old – only some few in the Close which are new built of
the Doctors houses by the Colledge and the Church.*

Celia Fiennes, 1698

Winchester, county town of Hampshire, was already an ancient
city when Alfred the Great made it his capital in the late ninth
century. The 'chester' in the name is a reminder of Roman
occupation, as are the arrow-straight roads that still lead into
the city from five different directions. The Romans established
a fort here in the first century AD shortly after they had invaded
England. Even then there is evidence of still earlier settlement.
Just to the south of the centre, there are traces of an Iron Age
hillfort on St Catherine's Hill. Its rampart and ditch probably
girdled a village that may have dated as far back as the fourth
or fifth century BC. The Roman army, under Vespasian, quickly
conquered southern England after the invasion of AD 43, and
that hillfort no doubt fell to his troops.

The early Roman fort seems to have been to the west of the
later town, though excavation opportunities to discover its
extent have been limited. Fortunately, in other parts of
Winchester, archaeologists have managed to piece together a
great deal of information about the city – often arriving at
surprising conclusions.

The Roman town was also a regional capital of the Belgae
tribe of Ancient Britons, and the Romans named it Venta
Belgarum – literally, the market place of the Belgae. By about
AD 100 a forum and basilica were built, just to the north-west
of the present cathedral, indicating that Venta was also an

2 For well over thirteen centuries, the cathedral has been a major factor in Winchester's history. This view from the east shows the great pile before its several nineteenth-century restorations. The accompanying text says that it 'was drawn from Dr Lowth's garden in the year 1781. The building seen on the south side, is his prebendal house.' That is No. 1 the Close, with the pediment, built in 1699.

administrative town. It seems that Winchester was always more of a regional centre than a military stronghold, even though its defences were improved over the years. Indeed, the much later medieval defences probably re-used Roman work.

Altogether the Roman walls enclosed 144 acres, making the town the fifth largest in the country. One of the more interesting finds by the archaeologists is that the rigid street plan within the walls that still survives today has little to do with the Romans. In fact, only the impressive straight road, well over half a mile long, from the West Gate to the bridge over the Itchen has Roman origins. For nearly two thousand years their *via principalis* has been the city's backbone. Other Roman streets, running at right angles to this one, have been discovered by excavation, but the remaining street pattern is Saxon.

For three hundred years or so, Venta Belgarum was one of

3 The Great Hall of the castle was spared the fate of the rest of its buildings after the Civil War. This view, published by S. Hooper in 1787, was copied from a painting of 1781 by Francis Grose. Comparison with the present appearance of the building shows how much work was needed in the nineteenth century to restore its medieval appearance. One major change, in 1789, was the demolition of the porch and the blocking of the original north door, replaced by one central to the elevation.

the principal cities in the province of Britannia and clearly prospered. How badly it was affected by the gradual disintegration of Roman power in the latter part of the fourth century is unknown, but by the early fifth century it would have suffered from the final withdrawal of the legions. The post-Roman economy, in the so-called Dark Ages, was rural, and urban life seems to have gradually petered out. As a marketing centre, Winchester might have fared better than most towns, but little is known about the city until the emergence of the new Saxon kingdom of the West Saxons – Wessex – in the sixth century. Some vestiges of urban life may have continued, and traces of buildings built across Roman streets have been found.

By the mid-seventh century the pagan West Saxons had been converted to Christianity and the first recorded church in Winchester was founded in about AD 645. In AD 662 Hedda,

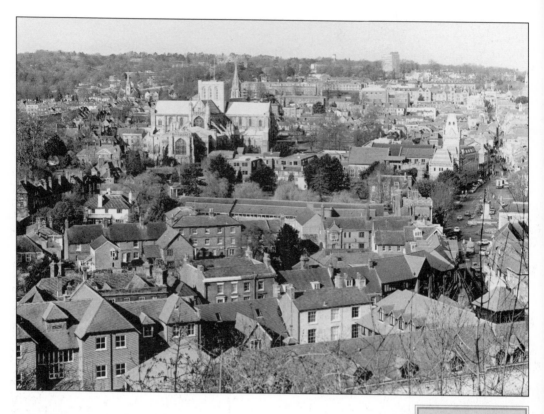

the bishop of the new West Saxon diocese, moved his cathedra, or bishop's chair, from Dorchester-on-Thames to Winchester, and the city's first cathedral was built. The Church has remained an important part of Winchester's life ever since.

In the ninth century Wintanceaster was the capital of Wessex, but whilst it contained the cathedral and the royal palace, there were probably relatively few houses other than those connected with the court. Saxon kings lived and were buried in the city, and a royal mint was established. This was also a period of increasingly damaging Viking raids, and Winchester was probably plundered in the middle of the century. Wessex held out – just – while most of the rest of England fell. Finally, during the reign of Alfred the Great, Wessex, and England, fought back.

One of the key elements in Alfred's strategy was the creation of fortified towns, or burhs, that could act as rallying points and defensive units in times of war, and also as constant

reminders to the Vikings of English power. The first series of burhs had been created before AD 892, and Winchester was one of them. Alfred knew Winchester well, probably grew up in the city, and was taught by its bishop, St Swithun. The city was also better placed than the important regional centre of Hamwih – now Southampton – which was particularly vulnerable to attack by sea. The Saxon scire of Hampshire was named after Hamwih, incidentally. Alfred's success led, inevitably, to Winchester's, and until the Conquest it was the royal capital of the united Saxon England – and only London vied with it for size and economic prosperity. A cult dedicated to St Swithun drew pilgrims to the city from the mid-tenth century onwards, and the cathedral, rebuilt and extended several times, became the largest north of the Alps. Winchester was a great centre of the arts and of learning – and its important buildings probably reflected this. It was also a place

5 For nearly two thousand years, the city's backbone has been the High Street, laid out originally by the Romans in the first century AD. This view looks eastwards, with the distinctive clock of the former guildhall on the right and Godbegot House on the left. In the middle distance is the Butter Cross.

6 The bishops of Winchester were men of substance and political importance in the medieval period. From their fortified palace, Wolvesey, they wielded tremendous power, unthought of by today's prelates. The medieval palace was destroyed after the Civil War, leaving only the small chapel intact. A splendid new palace was built in the 1680s – domestic splendour replacing defensive necessity. It was restored by William Douglas Caröe.

where the great political reforms begun by Alfred were worked out, and Edgar, the first recognized king of all England, standardized weights and measures based on those used in the city.

His son, crowned in the city in AD 979, was the unfortunate Ethelred the Unready. After the final defeat of the old Saxon order in the early eleventh century, the Danish king Cnut ruled his joint empire – stretching from Land's End to Scandinavia – from the palace at Winchester. The native monarchy returned in the shape of Edward the Confessor, crowned in the cathedral, but was defeated at the Battle of Hastings in 1066.

Within a month of their victory at Senlac, the Norman army arrived at the gates of the ancient capital of England. These were quickly opened and the city fell without a fight, allowing William to go on to take London – and the crown. Two years later, William the Conqueror came to Winchester to be

8 Because the cathedral was a monastic one, and the bishop spent most of his time travelling on diocesan or national business, the monastery itself was run by the prior. With the Dissolution of the Monasteries, the prior was replaced by the dean who still runs the day-to-day business of the church. Thus the thirteenth-century deanery, with its vaulted porch, was originally the prior's lodging. To the left is the fifteenth-century hall.

crowned for a second time. From then on, during every Easter that he was in England, he would stay at the royal palace by the cathedral and 'wear the crown' in a ceremony of great pomp and circumstance. William also ordered the building of a castle on the western edge of the old city, and then replaced the fine Saxon cathedral with a new one. The city continued to be a key part in Norman control of the country – the place where the original Domesday Book of 1086 was kept, along with the treasury and the exchequer. The Conqueror's inefficient son, William the Second (Rufus) was buried in the cathedral after the mysterious hunting accident in the New Forest. Only in the early thirteenth century did London become the sole place of government.

In its heyday in the mid-twelfth century, still bolstered by royal patronage and favour, the population of Winchester was well over 10,000, and possibly as high as 15,000 – huge

7 Opposite: This romantic statue of the great leader was erected in 1901 to mark the thousandth anniversary of his death. The sculptor was Hamo Thorneycroft.

numbers in medieval terms. The city had at least fifty-seven parish churches – only London had more – and towns such as York and Lincoln had fewer. Pilgrims continued to flock to the shrine of St Swithun, and the diocese stretched from London to the Isle of Wight. The church was also a centre of learning and the continuing tradition of high quality artistry led to the creation of the superb Winchester Bible begun in the first half of the century.

The city was a major marketing centre for the region, its fairs and markets attracting tens of thousands of people from all over the south of England. St Giles's fair, held on the slopes to the east of the city, was one of the biggest in Europe. The tolls paid to the bishop at the fair in 1189 amounted to nearly £150 – a figure difficult to put into a modern context. Winchester also became a centre of the wool trade, helped by its close proximity to good sheep rearing downland, and by the reliable and rapid river running in the valley. Weaving and dyeing shops grew up in the eastern part of the city and, on the river and several mill-races, fulling mills were built in which the cloth was beaten and stretched by water-powered trip-hammers. By the reign of Henry I the Winchester fullers had royal permission to form their own guild. Winchester was even something of a financial centre, much of this being in the hands of a large Jewish community now commemorated by Jewry Street.

Winchester continued to be an important political power base. During the civil war between Stephen and Matilda, the empress made the city her headquarters, being received in state at the cathedral in March 1141. Stephen's brother, Henry de Blois, was then the bishop and garrisoned his new fortified palace, Wolvesey Castle, to the south-east of the cathedral. Matilda's forces were based at the Norman castle to the west, and the city was caught up in the cross-fire between the two. The ancient royal palace by the cathedral was destroyed in the process. When more of Stephen's troops arrived in September, Matilda found herself forced to flee. Twelve years later the war was resolved by a compromise worked out by the bishop in Winchester which allowed Matilda's son, Henry II, to be Stephen's heir. Henry granted the city's first recorded charters – one to the guilds merchant and the other to the citizens.

9 The West Gate, seen from within the city in this mid-nineteenth-century drawing, has been one of the principal entrances through the walls since the Roman period. No one would dawdle with a hay cart today, despite attempts at 'traffic calming'.

10 A general view of picturesque Great Minster Street, looking towards the High Street. The tower belongs to St Lawrence's, a medieval church virtually hemmed in by later buildings – several hiding their timber framing behind brick, brick-tile or stucco façades.

Henry's son, Richard the Lionheart, was crowned at
Winchester – during one of his very few stays in England – in
1194. The unpopularity of his brother and successor, John, led
to a baronial rebellion, and to the arrival of Louis of France
and his army in England. In 1216 Louis took the city of
Winchester and the castle fell after a brief siege. In the same
year the powerful bishop of Winchester, Peter des Roches,
crowned the young King Henry III at Gloucester. He had a
great influence on the boy, and entertained him and the court in
Winchester. Later, Henry spent a great deal of money in
repairing the castle, the only legacy being one of the finest
medieval halls in Europe.

From then on, however, Winchester began a long and
lingering decline. A century later it was no longer even one of
the top ten cities of England. The importance of the St Giles's
fair waned after about 1300, and in the mid-fourteenth century
the city was hit hard by the plagues that ravaged England; the
population may have been halved. By 1377 it has been
calculated that Winchester was only just in the top thirty towns –
though such figures are always open to a great deal of debate.
Nevertheless, by the end of the fourteenth century, the city had
become a centre of purely local importance, with a population
of fewer than 3,000. Matters continued to get worse and in
1442 the citizens claimed in a petition to the king that nearly a
thousand houses and seventeen parish churches had fallen into
ruin in the past half century. Within the once crowded walls
there were now large areas of open space given over to
gardens, orchards and grazing. The western part of the city
suffered particularly badly, because this had been the more
fashionable area, close to the castle. The more industrial
eastern side, close to the river and the mills, fared slightly
better.

Despite this long drawn out decline, the cathedral was being
remodelled at great expense throughout most of the later
medieval period, and Winchester College was founded by
William de Wykeham, the bishop for most of the latter part of
the fourteenth century. In 1485 Henry VII's son and heir,
Prince Arthur, was christened at Winchester but, unfortunately,
died soon after his wedding to Catherine of Aragon. Even the
church was hit by the next round of misfortunes – the
Dissolution of the Monasteries ordered by Arthur's brother,

11 As this early 1900s postcard shows, Winchester has had a long connection with the British army – and still has. This is a view of the parade ground in the then recently rebuilt barracks by the castle. On the right the portico contains re-used columns and decorative masonry from the King's House, Charles II's unfinished palace, designed by Sir Christopher Wren.

12 Winchester's ancient Butter Cross is a reminder of the city's important role as a market centre – one that continues today. Essentially early fifteenth century in date, it was radically restored in the 1860s. The building to the right has a typical Winchester bow oriel window. The jettied, stuccoed, timber-framed building next to it includes fragmentary remnants of the Norman extensions to the Saxon palace.

Henry VIII, after he fell out with the Church of Rome. The cathedral's monastery was closed in 1538 and the cathedral refounded as a secular one; both Hyde and St Mary's abbeys were closed and demolished, and other smaller foundations were also lost or radically altered.

Briefly, royal pomp returned to Winchester in 1554 when Queen Mary married Philip of Spain in the cathedral, after staying at Wolvesey Palace. During the Civil War in the following century, Winchester, like most cities, tried to be aloof from the conflict. Indeed, in 1642 they had sent two MPs to Westminster – one Royalist and one Parliamentarian. This even-handedness was not matched by events, and the castle changed hands several times as first the Royalists and then Parliament gained the upper hand in Hampshire. In September 1645 Oliver Cromwell's forces attacked and quickly took the city; the 700-strong garrison in the castle held out for a week. Oliver's Battery, to the south of the city, is said to have been a Parliamentary artillery site – but is some way from the walls of the castle. Perversely, the city then became strongly pro-Royalist, especially when Charles I was held prisoner in the West Gate for a while in 1648.

Shortly after the Restoration of 1660, Charles II decided to build himself a palace at Winchester. Inspired by the French king's Versailles, it was designed by Sir Christopher Wren. The king had just finished a new palace at Windsor, and was deliberately snubbing the citizens of London who had treated his father so badly. For a while, it seemed that Winchester would again become, if not the national capital, at least the royal one. Charles loved the horse racing on the downs and the diarist Evelyn declared that the city was 'infinitely indeed preferable to New-Market, for Prospect, aire, pleasure, and provisions'. Work on the palace, the King's House, close to the great hall of the castle, began in 1682 and land was bought by the Crown in the city so that a huge boulevard could link it with the west end of the cathedral. The palace was almost finished when Charles died, but his successor, James II, immediately halted work. It was never finished, and the grandiose piece of townscape that would have completely altered the character of the city was left undone. Nevertheless, for a brief period, Winchester had once again been in royal favour and its economy had begun to pick up again – as

13 It is a little odd that buildings often become associated with people who hardly lived there at all. 'Jane Austen's House', 8 College Street, is one. She came here to stay with her sister Cassandra in May 1817 to be near the doctor treating her illness, but sadly died in July. She was buried in the north aisle of the cathedral.

14 26–7 St Swithin Street is reputed to have been the home of James, Duke of York, in the late seventeenth century. The building looks more of early eighteenth-century date and was clearly a substantial dwelling – the five-bay centre is flanked by short single-bay wings. Judging by the present two doors, it seems to have been sub-divided in the later part of the century and the ground floor has been altered since.

demonstrated by several fine houses of the late seventeenth century. Important improvements were made to the Itchen at around this time, which meant it was navigable for barges all the way up to Blackbridge Wharf by the city's east wall.

Although in the 1730s Defoe found the city to be a place of no trade and no manufacture, he commented on the abundance of good company and respectable society. Throughout the eighteenth century, Winchester continued to be a reasonably important regional centre and cathedral city, with its own 'season' for the local gentry. Despite this, it was dismissed as 'a paltry town and small' by Horace Walpole in 1755. The population had crept up to just over 6,000 by 1800 but little was to change for many years. In the nineteenth century it became the thinly disguised model for Trollope's sleepy but intrigue-ridden Barchester. Only in the second half of the century did the city finally become as populous as it had been

16 The Soke looks, from Chesil Street, like a large late Georgian house built of particularly dark red brick with bands of 'blues' at each floor level. The bulk of the house is of the seventeenth century, much of it in stone and possibly dating to 1609. The name is a reminder of the areas outside the Close, the Soke, once controlled directly by the bishop.

seven hundred years before and by the end of Victoria's reign it had over 20,000 people – scattered over a much wider area than their medieval predecessors had been.

Today the city retains its regional importance and, although having a population of well below 40,000, it is an important market centre for local agriculture and shopping centre for local people. Winchester's administrative role was strengthened in 1889 by the creation of Hampshire County Council, with its headquarters logically sited in the ancient county town rather than in the much more populous and successful coastal towns of Southampton or Portsmouth. This has also resulted in the siting of the county police headquarters in the city. Its famous college has a worldwide reputation and, above all, it is a well-known and much-visited tourist destination.

Top left: A fine early eighteenth-century doorcase with Corinthian capitals and a segmental pediment belonging to 12 Southgate Street.

Top right: The early nineteenth-century doorway to No 18 St Peter's Street, a house in a 'white' brick terrace.

Left: The door to Avebury House, St Peter's Street, is not the original and is probably a late Georgian replacement.

Architectural Character

The best way to appreciate the city is to do what thousands do each year – walk beyond the Broadway and climb up the flank of St Giles's Hill, scene of the great medieval fairs. Those who really are unable to do this the hard way can drive up the leafy lanes lined with the late Victorian villas that once threatened to engulf this fine open space – developments only stopped by public pressure. Today the view is a little tarnished by the tall office block on the opposite side of the valley – the county police headquarters built at the end of the 1960s. Its grounds are spacious enough – and there was simply no need to build it so high.

From the top of St Giles's, the city's position in the well-watered valley bottom can be better appreciated – as can the importance of the High Street. This is one of the longest, and most memorable, in England, dropping down from the medieval West Gate to the bridge over the Itchen by the City Mill. Since the Roman period this has been the spine of the city and still dominates its commercial life.

The gradual decline of the city from the thirteenth century onwards has left its mark on its architectural character. Perhaps unexpectedly, the ancient city walls were a fairly unimportant element in the way the city developed. No doubt at one time the area inside the walls was crowded with houses – so much so that suburbs grew up outside them. When the city contracted, it did not simply recede back into its defences. Instead, they were virtually ignored. Old maps show the High Street to be the main focus of later life, with housing also on

17 Today Winchester is a busy regional centre and is particularly popular with Hampshire shoppers. To cater for this, new shopping centres have been built, though their architectural attributes are somewhat questionable. In the Brooks Centre, opened in 1991, a bizarre mix of motifs and materials has replaced the austerity of the 1960s and '70s – but how will it look in twenty years' time?

The late Georgian tripartite doorway of 4 Kingsgate Street.

the nearest parts of the streets leading off it. The rest of the old walled city was virtually empty, apart from the area around the Close and the castle. Despite this, two of the suburbs continued to be well populated – the industrial eastern suburb around Chesil Street, and the suburb south of the city wall associated with the college.

For this reason, there are many historic buildings outside the old walls but in the areas immediately inside them – particularly to the north of the High Street – most of the housing is Victorian. Another by-product of the city's economic fortunes is that, although most old towns and cities would be expected to have grand houses throughout most of their centres, with lower class developments in the inner suburbs, Winchester tends to be a little contrary. Large houses are, as would be expected, around the Close and some along the High Street. Others turn up in the outskirts, notably the Georgian houses along Southgate Street

18 Several medieval towns have rows of houses with pavements running beneath them. What has actually happened is that, over the years, the buildings have encroached on the streets but their owners could not block the highway. The Pentice in the High Street is a good example, with timber-framed buildings mainly of sixteenth-century date. In the nineteenth century it was called the piazza.

and in Hyde. By the time Winchester was beginning to fill up again, in the nineteenth century, the wealthy were beginning to move to new villas in leafier outer suburbs. When this happened, large areas within the walls became available for new working-class housing – mainly terraces and semis.

All in all, the architectural feel of Winchester is a little uneven; apart from the most obviously important buildings in their distinctive settings, there are few places that can be described as being typical of, or unique to, the city. This variety makes exploring Winchester that much more satisfying – despite the occasional disappointments such as the large but uninspired late nineteenth-century houses connected with the college. These were built at a time when English architecture could be full of vigour and verve but, unfortunately, show the other side of that aesthetic coin. When Victorian architecture was bad, it was really bad.

19 No 9 the Close is one of the few early buildings in the city to be faced with ashlar. Probably built in the late sixteenth or early seventeenth century, it may well have used stone quarried from the redundant monastic buildings nearby. It also shows that symmetry was beginning to become an important factor in high-status house design. The sash windows are later modifications, of course, but there are some copies of the original cross-mullions. The porch is early Victorian.

Back on top of St Giles's Hill, looking down on this ancient city, most of its medieval set-pieces – surely one of the best collections in the country – can be picked out: the cathedral itself; the great hall of the castle; Winchester College; and Wolvesey Palace. Further down the valley is the hospital of St Cross. All these, and most of the churches, are built of stone – the most prestigious of medieval building materials.

However, Hampshire is not really a 'stone' county. In fact the local stone is not really a suitable building material at all – and certainly no good for the fine quality ashlar used in those grander buildings. The rolling downlands of the county are of chalk, and their thin soils are best suited to sheep. The rock itself is a very poor material for building with, and the best of Winchester's stone buildings are built of imported material. Only when there was royal or

21 A typical late medieval farmhouse stands at the northern end of St Cross, at the corner of Back Lane and Cripstead Lane. It has the characteristic wide panels, with braces and a jettied gable. The chimney stack is huge.

religious patronage could the expense of transporting such stone be readily met.

Much of the stone used to build the more prestigious buildings came from the Isle of Wight. Shipped from there across the Solent, it could be taken most of the way up the Itchen, navigable, with some difficulty, in flood during the medieval period. The best of these stones are two types of limestone quarried on the eastern side of the island. Quarr limestone was used extensively in the new Norman cathedral, and Binstead limestone was used in Winchester College. Much later on, both types of stone were used in Church House, in the Close – a rare example of a stone-built house in the city. Other imported stone includes sandstone quarried around Selborne used in the castle, and Purbeck 'marble' used in much of the internal decoration of the church at Holy Cross.

The only practicable building material associated with the local chalk was flint. Flints are small, hard, rounded nodules of

silica, often collected from the ground like pebbles and easy to carry to building sites. They are typically a rich, translucent black colour and can be worked in several ways. Used roughly they have little aesthetic value, but when halved and worked into more uniform shapes – 'knapped' – they can be used more architecturally. Because they are invariably small, and irregular, they need to be used in thick mortar courses and, more often than not, need good quality stone or brick for the strengthening of corners and openings. The Romans used flint in their town walls at Winchester, and were later copied by others – so much so it is often difficult to decide which parts of the walls were built when. Flint was a popular building material in the south-east in general throughout the medieval period, and enjoyed something of a revival during the nineteenth century. Its timeless quality could give an instant feeling of antiquity to the neo-historic buildings so popular during Victoria's reign.

23 Mobberley, in Kingsgate Street, is dated to 1571 and is thus the oldest brick building in the city. The red brick is decorated with burnt-headers in diamond (or diaper) pattern, and there are stone quoins on the corners of the main section and the surviving dormer gable to the left. Only one of the original moulded stone-mullioned windows survives – on the ground floor to the right – the sashes in the stone architraves being added during a Georgian remodelling.

Until the end of the eighteenth century Winchester was mainly a timber-framed town, and had been from the Roman period onwards. Archaeologists have discovered that the Romans lived mainly in timber-framed buildings covered over with plaster and resting on stone foundations. By the medieval period, a fairly standard way of constructing timber-framed buildings had developed throughout England.

The timbers were measured, sawn and cut in the carpenter's yard, and laid out into individual frames on the ground. Each important joint was cut, and the pieces temporarily slotted together. Each joint was then marked by a specific number – usually a type of Roman numeral – gouged or cut into the face. Then the frames were dismantled, and carted to the site. The numbers, or carpenters' marks, were to help the craftsmen on site put the frames back together again in the right order when

24 The narrow alley along the west side of Godbegot gives a rare glimpse into the crowded alleys of medieval Winchester. The first floor of the building is jettied out.

25 Fragments of the masonry of Wren's magnificent royal palace are on show in the Old Museum. This is one of the Ionic capitals. It may be the work of Edward Strong, employed by Wren at Winchester for making 'ornaments on several pilasters and carving ye tops of ye capitals'. He later worked for many years on St Paul's Cathedral, London.

26 English Gothic never really died. It lingered on after the end of the sixteenth century before being revived, at first whimsically in the eighteenth and then seriously in the nineteenth century. As a case in point, this Gothic window – essentially Perpendicular – is part of the gallery added to the deanery in the 1670s. Not surprisingly it is attributed to Sir Christopher Wren.

27 Hyde House, Hyde, is a mid-seventeenth-century building of brick, sporting this large Flemish end gable and a blank brick-decorated Ionic doorway. The brick bond is English: that is, alternating courses of 'stretchers' – bricks laid lengthways, and 'headers' – those with their ends showing in the wall face. It is now the Historic Resource Centre.

they were putting the building up. Once the basic carcass was up, the spaces between the timbers of the wall frames – the panels – had to be infilled to keep the weather out. This was usually done by creating a 'wattle' of twigs woven into a series of staves held between the top and bottom rail of each panel. Once the wattle was in place, a pungent mixture of clay and animal dung – the 'daub' – would be fixed to the wattle and, after it had dried, covered with a thin skim of plaster. In general, the earlier the framing the larger the panels.

Winchester has a good variety of timber-framed buildings of all periods but, as in most historic towns, many have been covered over when their owners decided to modernize. The main impetus for trying to hide the old timber frames was the rapid acceptance from the late seventeenth century onwards of brick. This allowed more simplicity of design and greater possibilities to achieve the symmetry and balanced proportions

28 No. 9 The Square has a Georgian front with a typical Winchester bow oriel and the house to the left has a tile-hung, late nineteenth-century gable with elaborate bargeboards. A quick look down the right-hand side reveals that it is, in fact, timber-framed and, judging from the braces and the large panels, probably of late fifteenth- or early sixteenth-century date.

29 A more obvious example of an altered timber-framed building is 23 Chesil Street, a late medieval building remodelled in the eighteenth century but once again with part of its framing on view.

30 This well-known bookshop at 19 The Square, close to the tower of St Lawrence's, looks typical of many other Georgian houses in the city. However, within is this late sixteenth-century timber framing.

31 Wren is said to have designed 4 St Peter's Street for Charles II's favourite mistress. The overhanging roof and general proportions would certainly support a date in the 1680s, but there is no evidence that Wren was involved. The house is of brick, and certainly would not have been stuccoed and painted bright white when built.

of the new neoclassical styles then being developed. Owners of timber frames who could not afford to rebuild in brick often just added brick fronts to their buildings, or simply covered them with render to create the illusion that they were more up to date than they looked.

Brick came relatively early to Winchester. One of the earliest brick buildings in the city is Mobberley in Kingsgate Street, dated 1571. Built of red brick, the original two-storey portion has two gables and stone quoins. The red bricks are decorated with a diaper pattern made of burnt brick headers. Nearly a century later, two parallel rows of three large brick-built terraced houses were built in the south-western corner of the Close. They were part of the rebuilding work needed after the devastation caused in the Civil War and the Commonwealth that followed it. The houses in Dome Alley are, in style, little different from the timber-framed buildings of fifty years

32 Minster House in Great Minster Street is a fine early eighteenth-century house of five bays under a hipped, overhanging roof with the modillioned cornices that were then so popular. It is good to see the sash windows have their glazing bars and that the house seems to be in tip-top condition. Winchester has more than its fair share of such buildings.

33 Canon Street is a pleasant Georgian street of unpretentious, mainly two-storey houses. All is not quite what it seems though, as the nearest building on the left-hand side shows. Despite its brick façade it is timber-framed. It is good to see that at least some thought has been given to the texture of the road surface – a great change from dull tarmac.

34 The fact that the
stuccoed upper storeys of
these Georgian-looking
houses on College Street
are jettied is enough of a
clue to give away their
timber-framed origins.
The buildings probably
date to the late sixteenth
or early seventeenth
centuries, and would
probably have been
remodelled in the later
eighteenth century.

earlier, but represent a confidence in the still uncommon building material. The bricks were actually made in the Close, and the houses were built by the cathedral's clerk of works, William Fletcher, in 1661.

Wren's use of brick for Charles II's great palace simply ensured the continued popularity of brick from then on. He also provided a perfect model for the simple neoclassical styles that would dominate domestic architecture for the following century. Because Winchester was then enjoying something of a boom period, it can boast many late seventeenth- and early eighteenth-century examples of fine brick houses.

For all of this period the bricks used were locally made and had a fairly cheerful red texture. The use of burnt-ended brick for decoration seen in Mobberley developed in the eighteenth century. Such bricks were used around window and door openings, in creating chequer pattern brickwork, and also in

35 This mid-nineteenth-century terrace of two-storey houses on North Walls also has a unified look, thanks to the central pediment. That bears a large plaque – now blank. Perhaps this was built by one of the many housing associations working around this period.

36 Owen Browne Carter was probably the best of the local architects working in the first half of the nineteenth century. In the late 1830s he designed this unified terrace with its Italianate undertones, 33–9 Southgate Street. There are four houses in the terrace, which is designed to look like one much larger house. Carter was probably also responsible for a nearby and almost identical terrace, Nos 41–7.

creating burnt-brick string courses. By the end of the century, yellow bricks – some types actually called 'white' – had been introduced. Because of their popularity in London, where they were the standard type of brick from the late-Georgian period onwards, these bricks became fashionable elsewhere in the south-east. The many examples in Winchester show that the yellow bricks were, for a time, considered to be better than the red – and buildings sometimes have yellow bricks on the front, and red bricks in the less important side and back walls.

Further varieties of brick became readily available with the advent of the railways, as, indeed, did varieties of stone. All this, in Winchester as elsewhere, helped to chip away at much of the local building character – a process accelerated by mass-produced materials. One characteristic that did survive through most of the eighteenth and nineteenth centuries was the use of

37 Symmetry found its way even to the humblest of Georgian buildings, such as these early eighteenth-century brick semis, 24–5 Kingsgate Road. The pair are designed to appear as a much larger house, sharing a central 'doorway' under a blind first-floor window. They were still given only casement windows at a time when any house of importance would automatically have been fitted with sashes.

38 The De Lunn Buildings on Jewry Street are a speculative development of houses above shops, designed by the local architect Thomas Stopher in about 1890. The design is certainly striking, though a little over the top.

the oriel bow window – the rounded, projecting windows clearly loved by the good people of this city.

The twentieth century has seen the rapid development of new building materials – concrete, steel, glass and plastic – and most buildings put up in Winchester in the past fifty years could have been built in any other town or city in Britain. The local style is effectively dead. It is also, unfortunately, true that there have been few good buildings built this century – and some real horrors. Included among the worst are the late 1960s extension to the county council offices; the police headquarters (for bad architectural manners more than for anything else); and, perhaps worst of all, the former Wessex Hotel on the north-east corner of the Close. Opened in 1963 it is truly awful; it would be bad enough if it were surrounded by landscaped gardens and sitting by the side of some motorway service station. But built on the edge of the greensward

39 This building in Kingsgate Street looks like a bit of Victorian fakery with its central pediment, stuck-on planking and 'Gothic' cornice. In fact, it is a genuine timber-framed building, probably of the sixteenth century, and its original jetty joists can still be seen in the centre. It was simply rendered and remodelled in the nineteenth century.

40 The sub-division of large properties into smaller ones has been going on in towns since time immemorial. The houses involved can often be adversely affected in the process. This corner property in The Square is part of the building to its right and the combined early Georgian town house would have been one of some pretensions.

41 One of the problems facing an architect when asked to extend an historic building is how it can be done without damaging the character of the original while not creating a pastiche copy. The problem was solved superbly in this complex in Middle Brook Street. The new build is definitely modern but allows the old, a late medieval range, due precedence; at the same time it has an almost Impressionist hint of medieval gables, jetties and timber framing. There are no gimmicks – and it shows an all-too-rare example of what can be done.

42 The recent restoration of the former Blue Boar Inn on St John's Street was, to say the least, unusual. The jettied, timber-framed building with its large timbers and large frame panels probably dates to the fourteenth century. When it was repaired, in 1970, the upper storey was reclad in uncompromisingly modern material – but the shape and feel of the original has been retained without resorting to 'stick-on' framing.

43 The new Hampshire County Records Office of 1993 is something of a rarity these days. The architect has at least had the courage to go with a positive design that doesn't rely too much on tacked-on detailing. Its spacious site on the periphery of the historic city made the job easier – and it will be easier for later generations to judge it objectively.

surrounding one of England's finest cathedrals, it is a planning disgrace. It is a sad fact that hotels, once built with dignity and pride, are all too often the worst of the new buildings in many historic cities. They may be well designed for their function, but they contribute nothing to the historic townscapes in which they lie and generally detract from them.

44 The West Gate was built in the thirteenth century, the last of a series of gates going back as far as the Roman city. This, the outside elevation, was remodelled towards the end of the fourteenth century. The loops were designed for what was then a lethal new weapon – the gun. Above, more primitive defence came from the machicolations below the parapet. Rocks and oil could be dropped on any unwelcome visitors trying to gain access through the gate.

Castle and Defences

Tracing Winchester's defences can be a little confusing. There were, in the Middle Ages, no less than four separate sets of defences: one civic – the walls around the city; one military – the castle defences; and two religious – the walls around the cathedral close, and those around Wolvesey – the bishop's palace.

The earliest defences in the vicinity are those of the old hillfort on St Catherine's Hill, just to the south of the city, but their remains are somewhat fragmentary. Nevertheless, the walk up to the top of the hill is well worth the effort just for the views over Winchester and the surrounding countryside.

The earliest Roman defences around Winchester were probably made up of a protective rampart, topped by a timber palisade and fronted by a ditch. On the east side the River Itchen seems to have provided sufficient deterrent for any attacker initially. Only later were the defences rebuilt in stone, probably at the very end of the second century AD when there was a political crisis in the province following the unsuccessful attempt by its governor, Albinus, to become emperor. The new defences included the eastern section on the west bank of the river. Fragments of Roman masonry survive in that section of wall, and no doubt much of the core of other sections of wall is also of Roman origin.

The Roman defences are not quite as regular as might have been expected. The line of the river might account for the odd alignments to the south-east, but at the southern end of the west wall there was a projecting portion of the defences that seems difficult to explain. It may be that the defences took

45 The Saxon and then medieval city wall followed the lines of the Roman defences, and no doubt the standing sections, although dating mainly to the thirteenth century, have a considerable amount of re-used Roman material within them. The main material is flint, roughly knapped and roughly coursed.

account of some existing building or shrine but the shape remains something of a mystery.

If the town's defensive circuit was fairly standard, there would have been a gate on each side. It is almost certain that the present West Gate stands on the site of the original Roman gate, and quite possible that the King's Gate is on the site of the original South Gate. The East Gate would have been by the east end of the Broadway, but the location of a North Gate is unknown.

After the departure of the Romans it is unclear whether or not the defences were simply allowed to fall into ruin. Recent archaeological evidence has suggested that some Roman fortifications were maintained from time to time during the so-called Dark Ages, and when Winchester developed as a royal and religious centre in the early Saxon period it is quite possible that its defences were kept in a reasonable state of repair.

46 The only other surviving gate in the city's defences is the King's Gate, south of the cathedral. It was probably built in its present form around 1300 and has a chapel, St Swithun's, on the first floor which is still used for services. This is the inside face, built of knapped rubble.

47 The Romans' early earth-and-timber defences around the city of Venta Belgarum were improved in the turbulent period around AD 200, being replaced by a wall of flint. This fragment in the eastern section – where there had been no defences before – is close to the Itchen.

48 Only fragments of the Norman castle remain on view, exposed again recently in excavations. The masonry in this view belonged to a round tower that replaced the original square one in 1222, shortly after the castle had been recaptured from the French Dauphin. The Great Hall is in the background.

Alfred the Great almost certainly repaired the walls after making Winchester his chief burh and the effective capital of Wessex. The walls seem to have protected the city in 1006 from the Danish army that pillaged much of modern-day Hampshire, but it appears to have surrendered to the same army a few years later when Saxon resistance throughout the country crumbled. The arrival of the Normans led to a similar, and perhaps swifter, capitulation.

The walls continued to be maintained and rebuilt for several centuries more. Most of the present surviving portions of city wall – the best portion being on the eastern flank – are faced with knapped flint and probably date to the thirteenth century. In the 1540s, John Leland wrote that the walls were complete and that he noticed six gates – North, East, South, West, King's and a small postern in the north-eastern sector. The gates still survived when Celia Fiennes visited in 1698, although a

49 Despite the loss of the rest of its buildings, Winchester's castle still has one of the finest medieval buildings in the country – Henry III's Great Hall. It took fourteen years to build, being finished in 1235. The central doorway is a later alteration. The medieval windows have 'plate' tracery and were once topped by their own miniature gables. The walls are a fairly irregular chequer of ashlar blocks and flint.

50 The inside of the aisled Great Hall is once again splendid. This postcard of about 1910 shows the interior as restored by Wyatt in the nineteenth century, but from 1938 to 1974 it was again encumbered with the paraphernalia of the courts. Hopefully that will not happen again.

century later all but two of the gates were pulled down to improve traffic flow.

The West Gate probably dates from the thirteenth century, although it was refaced in the late fourteenth century – possibly at the same time that work was being undertaken at the nearby castle. The gate-passage and east arch have typical Early English mouldings of early thirteenth century date, but the more important west face, which would have been seen by anyone approaching the city, is more decorative. The embattled parapets have gone, but the projecting machicolations – slots between the corbels underneath the projecting battlements – survive. These were originally a very practical design that allowed the defenders to drop rocks on to anyone attacking the base of the gate or wall, and became architecturally fashionable. The two arrow loops above the arch are not quite what they seem. They are, in fact, gun loops. Primitive artillery

52 A closer view of the buildings at Wolvesey, including the 'keep' with its typical flat Norman corner buttresses and central pilaster. These were built in ashlared stone to give strength to the coursed flint structure.

was becoming accepted in the latter years of the fourteenth century, but the accuracy and range of the new-fangled weapons was still somewhat suspect.

Traffic continued to drive through the West Gate until quite recently. Just before the Second World War the neo-baronial hotel that butted up against its north side was taken down ready for some traffic diversion, but cars were only finally banned from using the gate-passage in 1956. Recently restored, the West Gate houses a small museum, and affords fine views from its roof down the principal street of the city. The King's Gate is considered to be a little later than the West Gate, although the main arch could be of thirteenth- or fourteenth-century date. The ashlar stonework of the central portion of the ground floor is clearly earlier than the poorer quality work above. The two pedestrian arches on either side, with their brick heads, probably date to the eighteenth century. The gate is rare in having a chapel on the first floor that is still in use. Dedicated to St Swithun, most of its windows are quite small and appear to date from around 1500.

A key element in the Normans' swift conquest and continued control over their new subjects was the castle – a military device scarcely heard of by the Saxons. The Normans, wishing to control Winchester, quickly established one of their typical 'motte-and-bailey' castles within the highest portion of the defended city – the odd salient in the western line of the Roman walls. The walls were retained for defensive reasons and the work started early in 1067. The motte was a hurriedly constructed earthern mound, topped by a timber fighting tower; the bailey was a defended enclosure next to it. So crowded was the Saxon city that two streets and about fifty houses had to be demolished to make way for the castle.

Nothing is now visible of this first castle, although parts have been excavated in recent years – including a chapel built in the Saxon masonry tradition and including 'long-and-short' work on the corners. Little is left visible of the improvements to the castle that took place over the following centuries either. Part of the side of the footings of a solidly built square tower of the early twelfth century has been left open to view following recent excavations. Close by is the superb masonry of a round tower, complete with a sally-port, built in 1222 to replace the square tower. This work was begun by Henry III after the castle had been badly damaged during its capture by Prince Louis in 1216. The only substantial portion of the medieval castle still standing is also of this period – and it is one of the most magnificent medieval halls in Europe.

Before the new work could be carried out, older buildings had to be demolished and one of the men employed in this task was Gerard Le Mineur. Started in 1222, the Great Hall took nearly fourteen years to finish and cost over £500. The original master mason, a Master Stephen, used stone from Selborne in Hampshire, the Isle of Wight, Corfe in Dorset, and Bath – as well as some imported from Caen, in Normandy. In 1233 the walls were almost finished and supervision of the work was taken over by Elias of Dereham, who was also in charge of the new cathedral at Salisbury. Two years later the roof was completed and the Great Hall was finished. One remarkable feature of the hall is that in plan it is a perfect double-cube –

53 St Swithun's Gate leads into the Close from just inside the King's Gate. It was probably built in the fifteenth century, though on the site of an earlier one. Beyond are the timber-framed porter's lodge and Cheyney Court, both probably of late sixteenth-century date.

being 111 ft long and 55 ft wide. Such deliberate calculations were very rare in English medieval architecture – as seen by the many oddly-aligned buildings in castle complexes and cathedral closes.

The original trussed rafter roof was larger and steeper than the present one, dropping down to lower side walls. The original line of the top of the side walls was just below the tops of the medieval windows, each of which originally had its own steep-pitched gable. The main entrances to the hall were towards the eastern end of each side wall and joined by a cross-passage – and traces of the doorways can still be seen. The present main entrance was remodelled in 1845 in a sympathetic manner. The windows are fine examples of plate-tracery, in which the geometric shapes in the heads are carved out of large blocks of stone rather than, as later, being made up of lengths of moulded arches or ribs.

Inside, the Great Hall still retains a feel of its original Early English grandeur. As in a church, the central nave of the hall is separated from the aisles on either side by arcades of two-centred arches springing from the tops of splendid clustered columns of Purbeck 'marble'. The cross-passage was at the 'low' end of the hall; at the 'high' end there are still traces of a stone dais on which the king and his consort sat. Above the dais now is the famous Round Table – hanging on the wall but definitely built as a table. Sadly it is not the Round Table of King Arthur's Camelot, but was probably built for Edward I in the late thirteenth century. It is 18 ft in diameter, made of 121 separate pieces of oak, and weighs 1¼ tons. Henry VIII had the table repainted in its present form. Also in this end wall is a fine doorway, flanked by Purbeck columns, that would once have led to the private royal apartments. Over the years the Great Hall has been subjected to several alterations, particularly in the later fourteenth century when the roof over the aisles was raised and the windows lost their gables.

By that time the castle was no longer as important as it had once been. Edward I had carried out improvements to the defences in the late thirteenth century, but in 1302 he only just managed to escape a fire that destroyed the royal apartments. It was a sign of the city's gradual decline that they were not rebuilt. Instead, royal visitors stayed at Wolvesey, home of the bishops, from then on. By the time Henry VIII took the throne,

the Great Hall was kept in good repair, but the rest of the castle was being allowed to fall into dereliction and was gradually quarried for building materials. Hastily refortified during the Civil War, Parliament decided in 1649 to 'slight' it – that is, to ensure that it could never be used for military purposes again.

In the medieval period the Great Hall had been used for courts of law and from the mid-seventeenth century the assizes were held here as well as the quarter sessions. The hall itself was partitioned somewhat unkindly and remained so until the middle of Victoria's reign. In the early 1870s Thomas H. Wyatt designed a new court house to the east of the Great Hall and restored the hall itself, adding its present, rather fine, timber roof. Only the wall-plates, tie-beams, arch-braces and the arcading in the spandrels of the trusses are medieval survivals. The quality of Wyatt's work in restoring the medieval hall was not matched by his skill in building the new – and by 1938 the

54 Like those of many others up and down Britain, the precincts of Winchester's cathedral were surrounded by a defensive wall. The best-preserved portion is at the south side, along St Swithin Street. For some reason the saint's name in the street is spelt 'Swithin', while the gate to the Close at the end of it and the chapel over the King's Gate are spelt 'Swithun'.

buildings were in such bad condition that the courts moved back into the Great Hall and stayed there until 1974. Fortunately, the paraphernalia of legal furnishings – benches, docks, desks and tables – have once again been swept away. One nice recent touch has been the creation of a small medieval garden at the south side of the Hall.

Towards the opposite end of the city, the bishop also felt obliged to fortify his own residence, Wolvesey Palace. Worldly-wise and powerful, such prelates often had reason to defend their homes from a variety of enemies. Wolvesey was begun by William Giffard, William II's chancellor, in the early years of the twelfth century. However, most of the palace ruins visible today are the work of Henry de Blois, brother of King Stephen, carried out during the 1130s. The palace was finished just in time to protect the bishop from the wrath of Stephen's regal rival, the empress Matilda. The grounds of the palace are sited within the south-eastern corner of the city's defences, which were incorporated into the defences of the palace itself. To the west is part of the wall surrounding the Close, so the only new section of wall needed to complete a defensive perimeter was along the north side. The older portions of the castle or, more accurately, the fortified mansion, include the remains of a western hall, probably of Giffard's palace, a second hall built by de Blois, the gatehouse, a defensive keep and a garderobe tower. Later, the original Norman chapel was rebuilt in the late English Gothic style known as Perpendicular, probably in the fifteenth century. All bar the chapel was slighted by the Roundheads after the city fell in the Civil War. The bishops continue to live on the site, but in a new palace started in the year after Wren's King's House – and a very fine ashlar-faced Restoration building in its own right. The bishop's portion of the palace is not open to the public, but the ruins of the older portion are now managed by English Heritage and open during the summer.

The final set of defences once enclosed the cathedral and priory precincts, and the southern section along St Swithin's Street is particularly well preserved. At the end of this stretch is the one surviving gate, St Swithun's Gate, a quite plain though picturesque affair of the later fifteenth century. It has kept its original decorated doors and just inside is the timber-framed porter's lodge.

55 A close-up of one of the original nail-studded gates in St Swithun's Gate, with a pedestrian gate cut into it.

56 The splendid fifteenth-century reredos with its ornately housed statuary was an obvious target for the Puritan zealots in Cromwell's army and it suffered badly in the mid-seventeenth-century. It had to be heavily restored in the Victorian period. This is an early twentieth-century view.

Churches

In the twelfth century Winchester had just under sixty parish churches, many of which were probably of Saxon origin. At least eight pre-Conquest churches have been positively identified – though most remnants have only been found through excavation. One of the more interesting was that found in Tanner Street, St Mary's, thought to have begun life as a secular building in the ninth century before being converted into a church or private chapel a century later.

Pre-eminent among the Saxon churches, undoubtedly, was the Old Minster – the predecessor of the present cathedral and once one of the largest churches in Europe. The first church was probably little more than a palace chapel built for King Cenwalh around AD 645, but it would have been rebuilt when Bishop Hedda made it his cathedral in AD 662. Two hundred years later the saintly Swithun was buried outside its west door and pilgrims began to arrive at Winchester. The old cathedral was rebuilt again in the late tenth century and by the millennium was certainly the greatest church in Britain, if not in northern Europe. The lines of its foundations are exposed to view just north of the present cathedral and have been examined archaeologically to allow a reasonable understanding of the church's development.

After the Conquest the Normans set about the domination of both civil and religious life with some zeal, resulting in the almost complete obliteration of the finest specimens of Saxon architectural achievement. In 1070 the Saxon bishop of Winchester, Stigand, was replaced by one of William's royal chaplains, Walkelin, and nine years later a new cathedral was begun slightly to the south and east of the old, work beginning at the eastern end and progressing westwards. By 1093 the east end of the new cathedral was ready to be dedicated, and the bones of St Swithun were ceremoniously placed with honour within. The

57 The early fourteenth-century choir, shown in an engraving of about 1900. The ornate boxes on top of the later screens on either side within the arcades are mortuary chests, containing the remains of early kings, queens and bishops.

saint had been a humble man, and tradition has it that his displeasure at being moved led to a tremendous rain storm on the dedication day – and the old saying that if it rains on St Swithun's day it will rain for the next forty days as well. On the day after the consecration, the demolition of the Old Minster began.

The Old Minster was so called because of the founding of a second great church built alongside it from AD 903 onwards to serve a monastery founded by Alfred the Great. This became the New Minster. In places the two churches were only a yard or so apart and it was claimed that the singing of services in the one could be heard in the other – confusing the congregations. Not that far away to the east of the Old and New Minsters was a third great church, serving the nunnery founded by Alfred's wife in the late ninth century. Shortly after the Conquest the New Minster was resited just outside the north wall of the city at Hyde and the old buildings were pulled

58 The west end of the cathedral was being restored during 1993–4 and was sheathed in scaffolding. This is a postcard of the early 1900s. In many ways it is the least successful part of the great church, being designed shortly before de Wynford was involved in the remodelling work.

down. The Nunneminster was rebuilt by the Normans, and some fragmentary footings have recently been exposed at the back of the Guild Hall.

Winchester Cathedral, or more accurately, the Cathedral Church of the Holy Trinity, St Peter, St Paul and St Swithun, does not dominate the countryside in the way of the cathedrals of Salisbury, Norwich or Lichfield. It has no soaring spire or tall tower. In any case, it is sited in the fairly steep-sided valley of the Itchen and not even at the highest point of the city. Seen from either side of the valley, it is the sheer bulk of the cathedral that is so striking. Once becoming aware of it from the city streets, it is difficult to forget that it is there – the roof-line is almost insistent, seeming to go on for ever. It is, in fact, at 556 ft, the longest Gothic church in Europe.

Bishop Walkelin was clearly determined to show the defeated Saxons in their former capital that the Norman

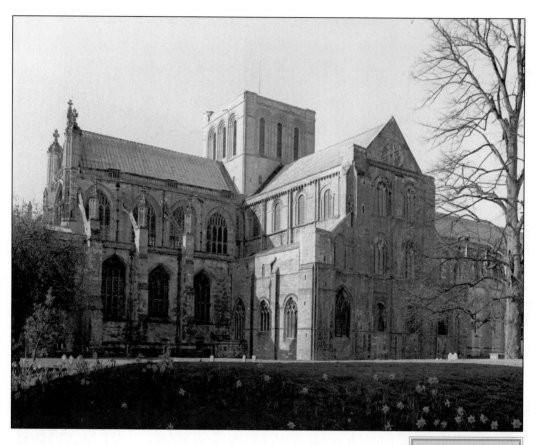

59 The great church built by the Normans to demonstrate both their power and their piety is substantially intact. It is only the details that have been altered. Most of the credit for that is due to the skills and architectural cunning of the master mason William de Wynford in the 1390s. This view, from the north-west, includes the north transept, the least altered section of the late eleventh-century work.

dynasty was here to stay and that the new order was better than the old. The cathedral was to outshine its far-famed Saxon predecessor and, indeed, virtually every other church in Western Christendom. There may also have been a deliberate attempt to show the king that Winchester was more worthy of being the capital than London.

The great Norman church, probably finished before the end of the eleventh century, may have been the work of one Hugh the Mason. It was built of limestone shipped from quarries on the Isle of Wight. The footings were laid on a huge raft of timber, because the ground was very wet. The church, though massive, had a fairly simple plan of aisled nave, a square crossing with the choir below a crossing tower, aisled transepts north and south, aisled presbytery with an apsidal ambulatory and, at the easternmost extremity, an eastern chapel with a rounded, or apsidal, east end. At the western end of the church

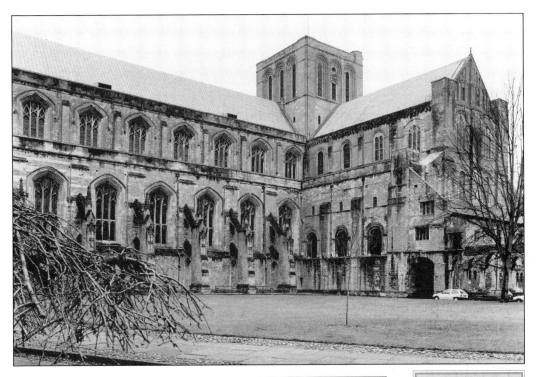

60 The monastic cloisters once stood to the south of the nave, but were swept away along with most of the claustral buildings in the later sixteenth century. At the extreme right is the arcaded entrance to the long-vanished chapter house. The Norman work in the south transept and tower is still clearly visible.

61 Winchester College Chapel, built by William de Wynford, was consecrated in 1394. Wynford then began work on the cathedral. This view dates to around 1900, and shows some of the college gardens.

there were probably a pair of towers flanking the main entrance. From the outside it is a little difficult to realize that the bulk of the church is still Norman, because of the later remodellings to its windows and doors. Inside, the same applies. It is only in the transepts that the early work survives little altered, clearly showing the scale and austerity of undecorated Romanesque architecture. A closer look at the arches of the arcade and triforium in the transepts show that something is not quite as it should be. The end arches by the crossing are somewhat abruptly terminated by the piers carrying the tower – even though these seem to be of the same style. The truth is that, despite the seemingly indestructible nature of the Norman work, the great central tower fell down in 1107 and had to be rebuilt.

Beneath the eastern end of the Norman church is a crypt, open only in the summer months because of the flooding that has plagued the cathedral. Its design clearly indicates the original shape of the eastern end of the Norman church. To the south of the nave was the cloister – because despite Walkelin's attempts to change matters, Winchester was a monastic, rather than secular, foundation, and in charge was a prior. Around the cloisters were the monastic buildings, including the chapter house and the dorter (or dormitory) on the east, and the frater (or refectory) on the south. Only the very plain arcaded entrance to the chapter house, and its north wall, are now clearly visible in this area, although a portion of the south-west corner survives encased in much later buildings.

Standing at the western end of the cathedral it is quite easy to forget its Norman origins and just to enjoy the splendour of one of the finest Gothic interiors in the world. What seems to be an example of the latest phase of English Gothic – the Perpendicular – is quite an ingenious remodelling of Bishop Walkelin's church. At other cathedrals, the older portions were often taken down and rebuilt afresh. This had been the case at the east end of Winchester when the beautiful retrochoir and Lady Chapel were built in the Early English style at the start of the thirteenth century, and when the chancel was rebuilt a century later. In each case, the Norman work above the crypt was demolished. In the mid-fourteenth century a different policy was decided upon. The masonry carcass of the Norman church was to be retained and reclad in new ashlar and redesigned.

62 The chapel of St Cross was built to serve the adjacent hospital founded by Henry de Blois in 1136. The tall church was begun in the late Norman style and finished in the early fourteenth century; the tower was rebuilt later still. The church thus contains work of Norman, Transitional, Early English, Decorated and Perpendicular periods.

63 The monastery founded by Alfred was moved away from its original site to a new one just beyond the North Gate in the hamlet of Hyde. As Hyde Abbey it prospered in the medieval period but fell victim to Henry VIII's commissioners. Although substantial remains survived at least until the 1790s, the only major surviving structure is the gatehouse. This is fifteenth-century work but incorporates older masonry.

The work was begun in the time of Bishop Edington, who demolished the Norman west end but recased the surviving cross-section of the nave and aisles with the masonry of the present west front. This is a very early, though not particularly impressive, example of the Perpendicular. Edington also began remodelling the west end of the nave, and the two lower windows at this end of the north aisle are a part of this work. The rest of the nave was remodelled in the time of his successor, William de Wykeham. The master mason responsible was William de Wynford, one of the greatest craftsmen of his time.

Work started in September 1394. One obvious difference between the nave of Winchester and the naves of most other cathedrals is that there are only two tiers of openings in the side walls, and not three. A brief glimpse into the transepts shows the normal arrangement of arcade, triforium and

64 King Alfred's wife founded the Nunneminster in the late ninth century. As its name suggests, it was a nunnery – a foundation to match the monastery, the New Minster, founded by the king. The nunnery, dedicated to St Mary, was rebuilt by the Normans but was pulled down after the Dissolution in 1539. Now only fragmentary footings remain, behind the guildhall.

65 There are other fragments of Hyde Abbey in the area, including this peculiar arch over the nearby mill-race that ran down through the abbey precincts. It was presumably part of a monastic building.

clerestory. Wynford was limited by the existing Norman masonry as to what he could do – and got around these restrictions superbly. The lower arcade and the triforium were effectively joined in the new work to form a much taller arcade between the nave and the aisles. Above, the large 'clerestory' window is not quite what it seems. Only the upper portions are truly windows – using the original Norman openings – and the lower sections are simply made of blind tracery. The play of light and dark, and the differing depths of the masonry, is quite splendid and so unlike the more mechanical Perpendicular churches that were to follow. The vaulting, which replaced the plain timber Norman roof, is of a complex type called lierne, and the ridges of each panel join to give a very strong emphasis on the sheer length of the nave. No doubt there were plans to remodel the transepts as well, but, perhaps fortunately, this work was never carried out.

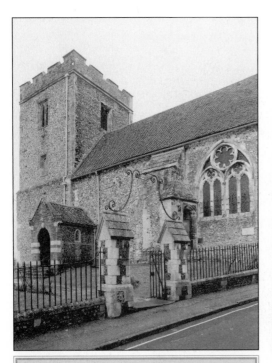

66 The church of St John the Baptist, in the suburb outside the eastern wall, is one of those very rare town churches that have not suffered at the hands of the Victorian restorer. It still retains the patina of antiquity. The south window of the aisle is a fine example of late thirteenth-century craftsmanship and design. To its left is the rood stair tower.

67 The other medieval church in the eastern suburb is no longer used for worship, but has found itself a role in the cultural life of the city as a theatre. St Peter Chesil is mainly of thirteenth-century date and has the type of pyramid roof on its tower that was once popular in Winchester. The masonry is essentially flint, but the top of the tower is tile-hung – probably an eighteenth-century modification.

Subsequent changes to the cathedral have been minimal. More vaulting was added over the next century or so, and the crossing tower was vaulted as late as 1634. By this time the priory had been suppressed and refounded as a secular cathedral, run not by a prior and monks but by a dean and chapter. The former prior's lodgings to the south of the cloisters thus became the deanery. The cloister itself and most of the monastic buildings had been pulled down in about 1570 and the materials sold off. The interior of the cathedral had been plundered by Henry VIII's commissioners, but far worse was to come during the Civil War when religious zealots vandalized most of the shrines and broke most of the stained glass. Most of the modern glass is dull and Victorian. The medieval glass would have added great colour to the inside of the church, matching the bright wall-paintings that covered most flat wall surfaces.

68 To the south of the city centre, off the Culver Road, is the church of St Michael's, the typical pyramid-topped tower of which dates back to the fourteenth or fifteenth century. Some old masonry survives in other parts, but the church was virtually rebuilt in the 1880s by William Butterfield.

A fragmentary set of these survives in the Holy Sepulchre chapel in the north transept. Fine as they are, it is perhaps easier to appreciate the sheer quality of the architecture of our great cathedrals in their present, unpainted, post-Reformation state.

As with all medieval churches, the cathedral has needed constant repair and maintenance. The first major restoration was carried out over a number of years in the early nineteenth century by William Garbett. The west face was restored in 1860 and then, for nearly twenty years from 1871 onwards, local architect John Colson carried out a series of repairs costing in excess of £40,000; during that time Gilbert Scott worked in the chancel. At the start of the twentieth century came the most dramatic restoration of all; the timber raft on which the Normans had built the church was in a bad way and the whole fabric seemed in danger of collapse. Sir Thomas

70 A detail of the south door of St Bartholomew's, probably part of the Norman work of the early twelfth century.

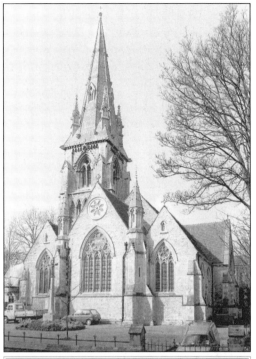

71 The old medieval church of St Clement's was replaced by a new one dedicated to St Thomas and St Clement by 1846, the spire being added in 1857. No longer a church, it was until recently used as the county's records office.

Jackson was called in to supervise the work – but it was the gallant efforts of the man who has gone down in folklore as the saviour of the cathedral that attracted the public eye. Diver William Walker, whose statue stands in the cathedral, spent several years in the waterlogged timbers and cleared the way for Jackson to underpin the footings with concrete. As part of the same work, buttresses were added to the south wall of the nave aisle – paid for by sponsorship. The 900-year-old church is again the subject of a major restoration programme, the tower having been dealt with recently and the west front being repaired currently. It is a never-ending task.

The only substantial remains of the resited New Minster, rebuilt outside the walls in about 1110 and generally known as Hyde Abbey, is the gatehouse. This is not the original, and probably dates to the fifteenth century, but could be a remodelling of an older structure. The monastery was closed in

1538 and its property taken by the crown. Many more buildings, though ruined, survived until the later eighteenth century, but apart from the gatehouse there are only a few intriguing arches over the adjacent mill race and clear signs in nearby buildings of re-used stone taken from the abbey.

To the south of the city centre is another fine example of Norman work altered by later craftsmen. The church of St Cross is best seen from across the Itchen water-meadows, but the tranquillity of the setting is ruined by the constant roar of traffic on the bypass. Despite its sheer size, this was to be simply a chapel serving the hospital of St Cross founded by Henry de Blois in 1136 in the village of Sparkford. The hospital was founded to house thirteen poor men who were 'feeble and so reduced in strength that they can hardly or with difficulty support each other with another's aid' and, as a side-line, to provide a hundred poor men with a daily meal. The cruciform church is surprisingly tall for its length and in its flat, unencumbered setting is more impressive than the cathedral.

Work on the church only seems to have begun in about 1160, and the last major additions to it – the nave vaults – were not finished until the start of the fifteenth century. The chancel was finished in about 1171, and the crossing and transepts by 1200. Work on the nave continued in two main campaigns, one in the first half of the thirteenth century and another a hundred years later. The overall result is a very important example of how the Norman style of architecture evolved into the English Gothic. By the time the church was started, the austerity of the early Norman work had given way to a much more decorative approach which paved the way for the Early English style seen in the later parts of the nave. More remarkable are the triforium arcades of the chancel – thought to be influenced by the classical architecture Henry de Blois had seen on his journey to Rome in 1151. The church was radically restored by William Butterfield in the mid-1860s, but its essential character remains; it is an architectural textbook in stone.

To the north of the church is the oldest surviving almshouse foundation in England – though by no means the first to have been founded and not even the first or the largest to have been founded in Winchester. The quality of the church and the rest of the buildings owes much to the royal connections of its

72 Ten years after the church of Holy Trinity was finished, Henry Woodyer built the vicarage nearby in a matching medieval style. It is an original and striking composition that included a first-floor 'medieval' hall. Later alterations, though minor, have not been kind.

patrons. Henry de Blois was a half-brother of King Stephen, and Cardinal Beaufort, who effectively founded a second almshouse on the same site, was half-brother to Henry IV. The collegiate form of the hospital is similar to that of Winchester College. The original layout is unknown, and most of the present buildings date to the refounding of the hospital by Beaufort in the mid-fifteenth century. They consist of an outer court reached through a gateway. A second gateway through the base of a tower leads into the main quadrangle, with the brethren's lodgings on the west side, the hall and master's lodgings on the north side, and, until the late eighteenth century, a south range of lodgings between the west range and the church. The attractive timber-framed east range had the infirmary above and a covered walk or pentice below; it was added in the early sixteenth century. In the late seventeenth century Celia Fiennes explained the famous tradition of

St Cross 'dole' – 'by their foundation they are to give relief to any Travellers that call there so farre as a Loafe of bread . . . and a Draught of beare and a piece of money, I thinke its value of a Groate'. This is still 'doled' out to travellers – but only those who arrive early can be certain of refreshment!

Much older than St Cross though far less intact is the former St John's Hospital in the High Street, described in the 1540s as 'a fair hospital . . . wher pore syke people be kept'. Its chapel was remodelled, probably in the fifteenth century judging from the Perpendicular motifs, but was likely to have been built two hundred years before that. It is immediately to the east of St John's Hall. That in turn is a remodelling of the medieval thirteenth-century hall of the hospital, and behind there seems originally to have been a double-aisled building not dissimilar to St Nicholas's hospital in Salisbury. The rest of the extensive hospital buildings, on both sides of the street, are mainly of nineteenth-century date and are used as almshouses.

By the start of the nineteenth century Winchester had just nine parish churches. From then on there was a steady increase as new churches were built (and old ones rebuilt) to serve the growing population. The use of flint, with its instant antiquated appearance, allowed architects of the Gothic Revival to blend in their new buildings with the old, and their rebuildings seldom look as ill-conceived as they often were in other towns and cities.

In the former industrial suburb to the east of the city is the parish church of St John's. In the nineteenth century this was a poor part of the city and was clearly unable to support any rebuilding work. The oldest portions of the church are two arcades possibly of late twelfth century date. A little later are a pair of thirteenth-century lancet windows, with fine wall-paintings, rediscovered in 1958. Also of the late thirteenth century is the fine window of the south chapel off the chancel, a good example of the early Decorated style of Gothic. The rest of the church seems to have been remodelled in the fifteenth century and is basically Perpendicular. It still has its rood-loft stair jutting out from the south wall; rood lofts were an important part of the church's liturgy before the Reformation, after which most were ripped out by the reformers. The attraction of the church is that all these historic elements remain unaffected by architectural tidying – the

73 The new St Peter's Roman Catholic church, despite appearances, was built as late as 1926 to the design of Frederick Walters. The revived Gothic style in this case is the middle period – the Decorated. All in all it is a very satisfying composition of ironstone rubble and Bath stone dressings.

church's development is organic and piecemeal, and none the worse for that.

Just to the south of St John's is the former church of St Peter Chesil, mostly of early thirteenth century date, with an attractive tile-hung tower. Like several churches in the area, this is topped by a squat pyramidal spire. Since the 1960s St Peter's has been turned into a theatre workshop.

To the north of the city the former hamlet of Weeke is now a part of Winchester. St Matthew's, its tiny church, looks, from the outside, to be of seventeenth century date but the bulk of the masonry is Norman – including the chancel arch.

Two other medieval churches in the suburbs have undergone quite radical alterations. To the north of the entrance to Hyde Abbey is the parish church of St Bartholomew, almost certainly built not long after the monks of the New Minster were relocated to the area. To an early Victorian writer the church

was 'well adapted to the accommodation of all the parishioners . . . [but] . . . not entitled to particular architectural notice'. Norman masonry and arcades, much restored, survive within. The tower is later, of flint and ashlar chequer – and topped by the pyramidal spire. The chancel was completely rebuilt by John Colson in the late 1850s – the flint looks the same as the older work but the ashlar trimmings are much crisper and less weathered. Much of the north side of the nave was rebuilt in about 1880.

Between Kingsgate Street and Culver Road is the much rebuilt church of St Michael's. The tower is probably of fifteenth-century date, but the rest of the exterior is mainly the result of work by William Butterfield in the 1880s. He, in turn, was remodelling an earlier nineteenth-century restoration. A projected north aisle, to replace one pulled down in 1822, was planned but not finished.

74 Henry Woodyer was perhaps not one of the great Victorian church architects and some of his work is decidedly dull. However, he did have his own way of doing things and Holy Trinity, opened in 1854 in North Walls, is arguably one of his best.

There are two curious churches in the centre of the city with medieval origins but only their towers showing. In Great Minster Street, almost completely hemmed in by later buildings, is St Lawrence's. Only the west tower is clear of the throng and probably dates to the fifteenth century. The church was badly damaged by fire in 1978 but has been restored. Another tower stands a few hundred yards to the east, but this one has lost the rest of its church. There is some doubt as to the date of this fragment of St Maurice's as the medieval church was radically restored by William Glover in 1842. It is likely that it does have medieval masonry within it.

From the mid-nineteenth century onwards Winchester, in common with other towns, experienced something of a religious revival accompanied by the construction of new churches. The old medieval church of St Thomas in the wealthy suburb centred on Southgate Street was pulled down –

75 The Baptists seem to have followed the neoclassical traditions of Nonconformist chapels more strictly than other groups who often veered, eventually, to the neo-Gothic of the established church. The stuccoed Winchester chapel, on City Road, is Italianate in style and was presumably built in the middle of the nineteenth century.

as its near neighbour, St Clement's, had been centuries before. A competition was held to choose the architect of a new replacement. In 1844 this was won by Webbe of London but there were clearly problems and when work started in the following year, the architect was E.W. Elmslie. Finished by 1846, St Thomas and St Clement's is a good example of the early Gothic Revival. The broach spire, such a feature of this part of the city, was added in 1857. Until recently it was used by the County Records Office.

Holy Trinity on North Walls is a fairly plain, flint-faced church in Henry Woodyer's own brand of Gothic. Opened in 1854 the essentially Decorated style church lacks a tower; only a spindly spirelet breaks the monotony of the roof structure. The decoration above the east window is an unusual touch. Nevertheless, it is a crisp and clear composition, with a surprise inside. The walls are ablaze with paintings of the Stations of the Cross by Joseph Pippett, added in the 1880s. On the junction of North Walls and Upper Brook Street is the excellent vicarage designed and built by Woodyer ten years later but sadly altered unsympathetically since.

Another architect with his own distinctive style was an Evangelist, the aptly named Ewan Christian. He designed Christ Church, on the Christchurch Road, opened in 1861. It has a tower topped by another broach spire and a spacious interior.

One Victorian church took nearly forty years to complete. The area to the west of the new railway developed rapidly in the second half of the century and a new church, St Paul's, was begun at the start of the 1870s. The architect was local, the elder John Colson. In 1872 the chancel was finished and dedicated. By 1889 the nave and transepts were ready but the final aisle was only finished, by Colson's son, in 1910 – by which time religious fervour was in serious decline.

The last of this set of churches to be started was one of the final works of John Loughborough Pearson, the designer of Truro Cathedral as well as many other churches. All Saints, in the Petersfield Road east of the city, was finished in 1898 – the year after he died. Actually, it was never really finished – the planned tower was abandoned.

Until the time of Henry VIII, all of the churches in the city were, of course, Roman Catholic. After the religious turmoil of

the mid-sixteenth century, Catholics in England were persecuted for several centuries and not allowed to worship freely or publicly. In the early part of the century, Defoe hinted that there was a semi-secret Catholic group centred on Hyde House and the ruins of Hyde Abbey who got on well with their Protestant neighbours. Perhaps it was this tolerance that allowed them to build, in Winchester, what is claimed to have been the first Roman Catholic church in England to be consecrated since 1558. Tucked away in a courtyard off St Peter's Street, and opened in 1792, it is also considered one of the earlier attempts at a more serious revival of medieval Gothic. It was designed by John Carter, an important figure in the late eighteenth century for trying to make people aware of England's medieval heritage – though more noted for his books than his buildings. The church, dedicated to St Peter, was largely paid for by John Milner. Oddly, the church that has

76 The former Roman Catholic church off St Peter's Street, built in 1792, is claimed to have been the first to have been consecrated in England after 1558. It is also seen as one of the very early attempts at Gothic Revival – although its stuccoed façade, thin buttresses, tall battlements and narrow tracery are still more reminiscent of the lighter 'Gothick' of the mid-eighteenth century.

77 The spiky United Reform church on Jewry Street was built as the Congregationalist church in 1853. That in itself is not unusual. What is unusual is its relationship to the buildings on either side. Both of those are part of the former gaol, and the church was built on another section of it in between the two.

replaced this pioneering example of the Gothic Revival is an exceptionally late, though more developed, version of the same, completed as recently as 1926. The architect was Frederick Walters. Despite such a conservative style, this large church of ironstone rubble with Bath stone decorations is rather fine, and its tower a good contribution to the cityscape. It contains a much-travelled Norman doorway, said to have originally come from the hospital of St Mary Magdalene, suppressed during the Reformation. This door had been re-used in the entrance-way to the first Roman Catholic chapel, and then reset once more in the new church.

Nonconformity has been around in Winchester for centuries but doesn't seem to have thrived until the latter part of the nineteenth century. Its architectural legacy is varied. One of the better examples is the United Reform church, built on to part of the old gaol on Jewry Street in 1853 as a

Congregationalist church by W.E. Paulton. The church cost £2,500 to build and boasts a double hammer-beam roof. Further north, on City Road, is the stuccoed nineteenth-century Baptist chapel.

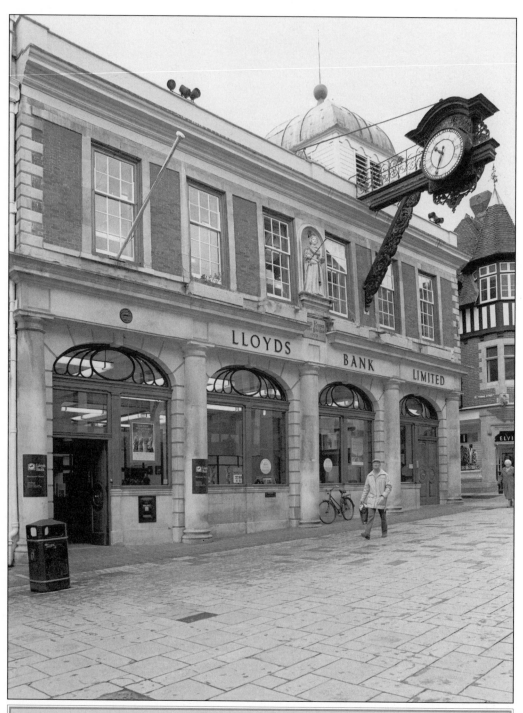

79 The earliest record of a guildhall – or hall of court – on this High Street site was in the late thirteenth century. This bank was built as the new guildhall in 1713 and originally had an open ground floor. The clock is a modern replica of the old, made by a local man, E. Laverty.

Public Buildings

Winchester has been an important administrative centre for most of the past two thousand years, and has a wide variety of public buildings that reflect this – though most are quite recent and the quality of their architecture is extremely varied. For centuries, administration of the county of Hampshire was carried out in the medieval castle. Now only the Great Hall survives and that is no longer used for the courts. However, tradition has died hard, and most of the major administrative buildings have been built on the site of the castle and in the adjacent areas. Together, these buildings provide a vivid demonstration of English architectural fashions in the hundred years between the 1890s and the 1990s.

Castle Avenue, the approach from the Upper High Street to the entrance of the Great Hall, is a suitably impressive piece of streetscape. The roadway has been cobbled and the buildings flanking it, largely faced in flint, are of fitting scale, texture and design. None is particularly old – the road itself only being created in 1896. In the mid-1870s Thomas Stopher had designed buildings on Castle Hill for the Hampshire Friendly Society. Shortly after being created, Hampshire County Council purchased these buildings in 1890 and then employed Sir Arthur Blomfield to extend them in a neo-Tudor manner. This eastern row, the Castle Hill offices, was finished by 1893. On the opposite side of the road further buildings in a similar vein were added in 1912 to the designs of Sir Thomas Jackson, and an additional link block added as late as 1931–2 by Sir Herbert Baker. All are of a fairly uniform design, one given a sense of antiquity by the flint-knapping used and the styles chosen.

Only a few years after the last of these ranges had been opened, a very different design had been chosen for more offices on the opposite side of the High Street close to the West Gate. The architect chosen was C. Cowles Voysey and plans were ready in 1936. The imminent start of the Second World War halted work, however, and the buildings were not ready to be opened – by the new queen – until 1959. The design was thus already twenty years old by then. It was also dramatically dissimilar to anything else in the complex – tall and faced in brick with obvious Dutch influences. It is a fairly attractive building in its own right, but perhaps a little too large for its simplicity.

By the end of the 1960s yet more office space was needed and a new extension – a bland, boring and bad-mannered block of no architectural merit whatsoever – was tacked on to the north end of Voysey's building. The difference in the quality

81 The county council offices designed by Cowles Voysey in 1936 were totally different from those on the opposite side of the main road. Tall, brick and symmetrical, they were influenced by continental design.

82 The new Crown Courts were built to the east of the Great Hall between 1965 and 1974. The Louis de Soissons Partnership were the architects. The design is uncompromisingly modern but in its own way echoes the bay pattern of the medieval building. The use of materials is also rather good. The worst part of it is the link block between medieval and modern – totally unworthy of either.

of the designs is huge. At the same time, new Crown Courts were being built on the site of Wyatt's short-lived building to the south of the Great Hall. These are by the Louis de Soissons Partnership and opened in 1974. The design is uncompromisingly modern but at least tries to reflect a little of the bay pattern of the Great Hall. The bland brick link between the ancient and the modern is the most disappointing element in the composition.

Further new extensions were needed in the mid-1970s, the Donald Insall practice being chosen as architects. Although the retention of a fine Georgian house of quiet distinction on Trafalgar Street, and most of the five large Victorian houses on the High Street is to be applauded, the design of the new build is less satisfactory. True, fashions change, but the buildings lack sparkle, are beginning to look rather tatty, and have the ugly, leaded 'Mansard' type of attic storeys so

83 The present Gothic guildhall on the Broadway was designed by Jeffery & Skiller and opened in 1873. Despite its Gothic trimmings, it is really a logical and symmetrical building. The later extension to the right, containing a school of art, was unfortunate. Considering Winchester's medieval role as a wool town, it was perhaps appropriate that the design was clearly influenced by the great thirteenth-century cloth halls of Ypres and Bruges.

84 The Victorians liked their gaols to be substantial, solid and grim – and the county gaol in Romsey Road is no exception. Designed by Pearse, it opened in 1850.

85 The prison on the Romsey Road replaced the old one in Jewry Street, where there had been a prison for centuries. It had been remodelled by George Moneypenny half a century previously, influenced by Dance's Newgate.

86 Arguably one of the finest provincial public buildings of its time, the former Corn Exchange in Jewry Street is now the city's library. Designed by Owen Browne Carter it opened in 1838 but its corn factoring days were short-lived. It is now a library.

popular in the period – an architectural equivalent of flared trousers.

In some ways the most recent additions are worse. At least the 1960s and '70s buildings had a degree of integrity about them. Close by the Voysey range is Mottisfort Court, an unfortunate exercise in the presently fashionable pseudo-vernacular-cum-postmodernist style that seems to want to please everybody and fails to satisfy anybody.

One of the most distinctive features of Winchester is the huge bracket-held clock on a High Street bank. The clock is largely renewed, but the original was given to the city in 1713, along with a statue of Queen Anne. The building itself was the former guildhall, built in 1711–13 on the site of an earlier building – and a fine example of the late English Baroque. Originally the ground floor was an open arcade. It is from the large weather-boarded turret above this building that the curfew bell is tolled every evening at 8 p.m., just as it has been since the eleventh century.

At the far end of the High Street, on the Broadway, is the city's present guildhall. A competition for the design was run in 1870, the winners being the little-known practice of Jeffery & Skiller of Hastings. Their design was a bold Gothic one based on splendid European examples – and the cost was over £10,000. The symmetry of the composition, and much of its dramatic effect, was lost when an extension was added to the east to the designs of John Colson in 1893. It is too plain and too tall – and presently unused.

Being a royal city and home of the courts also meant that Winchester had its prisons. In fact, it still has its prison, just outside the city centre on the Romsey Road. This was built to the design of a Mr Pearse and opened in 1850. The forbidding stuccoed gateway is now largely obscured by more hi-tech defences, and the central tower is best seen from a distance. This county gaol replaced one that had been on the same site in Jewry Street for centuries. Substantial remains of the last remodelling of that prison are still there in the streetscape – though very difficult to spot. The large, yellow-brick, pedimented, five-bay front of 11a Jewry Street, next to the United Reform church, was the central portion of a façade to the prison designed by George Moneypenny in about 1805. On the other side of the church is another part of that same face,

87 Close to the former Corn Exchange is the Theatre Royal, built as the Old Market Hotel in the late Victorian period but converted into a theatre in the early twentieth century and refaced.

88 The Old Market House, or Green Market, was built by the city engineer, William Coles, in 1857 at a cost of just £1,200 for the sale of fruit, vegetables and poultry. It was rebuilt in its present form in 1958.

the north angle pavilion, once containing the debtors' dining room. The site of the gaol had been sold off in lots – some new owners keeping and adapting parts of the prison building, others knocking them down.

There are several reminders of Winchester's continuing role as a marketing centre for local agricultural produce. By far the oldest is the famous and much-photographed Butter Cross, at the north end of the Pentice in the High Street. Originally built in the first half of the fifteenth century, it should really be called the High Cross or the City Cross – the present name apparently started being used in the early nineteenth century when traders in dairy produce sold their wares around it. The present appearance owes a great deal to a restoration by the famous Victorian architect George Gilbert Scott in 1865. Of the statues only that of St John, on the south side, is medieval. In the late eighteenth century, the Cross was in grave danger of being demolished as part of a long-term programme of improving the roads and streets of the city. Vehement opposition from the citizens prevented this going ahead.

The city has one of the most attractive libraries in Britain, housed in the former Corn Exchange on Jewry Street. It is a low Italianate building of yellow brick, with low-pitched overhanging roofs and a fine portico said to have been copied from Inigo Jones's church of St Paul's, Covent Garden. The architect was a local man, Owen Browne Carter, and the building, costing about £4,000, opened in 1838. It was, quite rightly, praised at the time as being 'a considerable ornament to the town – as well as being a very commodious and convenient market'. By the early twentieth century part was being used as the Regent cinema, but in 1936 the buildings were converted into the city's main library. The outside was sympathetically restored in 1964 and the inside was remodelled in 1977.

The much altered remains of another market building lie on the south side of the High Street not far from the cathedral. The Market House with its Greek Doric columns and red brickwork was designed by the city engineer, William Coles, and opened in 1857. This was the Green Market where poultry, fruit and vegetables were sold.

Care for the sick, the poor and the needy in the medieval period was the moral responsibility of the church but after the

89 Winchester College was founded on land just south of the city wall by William de Wykeham in 1382. The main entrance is off College Street, through the original outer gate. To the left are the warden's lodgings, medieval but raised and remodelled in the early eighteenth century.

90 The small museum at the north-west corner of the Close was begun in 1902 and holds some good displays on the city's history – being particularly good on the archaeology of buildings.

Reformation these unfortunates had to rely on their own resources or on charity. Winchester built the first public infirmary outside London, founded in 1736 due in the main to the efforts of Canon Alured Clarke. The present hospital on Romsey Road – renamed the Royal Hampshire County hospital – is a huge Gothic polychrome brick pile designed by the prolific William Butterfield. Built between 1864 and 1868, it is presently undergoing extensive renovation work.

In the eighteenth century Winchester had a purpose-built theatre on Jewry Street but the last vestiges of this have now disappeared. The present theatre, a little to the north and on the opposite side of the same street, started life as the Old Market Hotel in the late nineteenth century. Early this century it became in turn a music hall and then a theatre, used, from 1920, mainly for films. The florid front dates from about this period and, although hardly a superb example of theatrical architecture, it is always good to see a theatre still open and apparently thriving.

Winchester is, of course, noted for its famous public school, Winchester College – one of the oldest in the country. The church had long been an important provider of education in an age when most people, even the aristocracy, were illiterate. The education provided by the church was not given simply out of altruism – both church and state needed educated administrators. All this teaching was fairly loosely organized, which is why Winchester College was such an important development in the education system. William de Wykeham became Bishop of Winchester in 1366 and remained so until his death in 1404. At Oxford he founded New College, and at Winchester he founded a college on similar lines in 1382 that would prepare boys to go to the University. At first the seventy boys were lodged in temporary accommodation in the Chesil Street area and used St John's church as their chapel while the new buildings to the south of the cathedral close were being built.

Work on these began in 1387 and the majority of the buildings were ready by the time the chapel was consecrated in 1394. The master mason was, perhaps not surprisingly, William de Wynford who was already well known to Wykeham and would later remodel the cathedral. Much of the medieval work around the two main courts – the outer court and the

91 Next to the college's outer gate is the headmaster's house designed by George Repton and finished in 1842 – certainly not one of his better works.

92 The Pilgrims' School is far more homely than the college. It was only founded in 1931 and is housed in a pleasant, late seventeenth-century house in the Close. The left-hand wing, of flint rubble walls, incorporates the medieval Pilgrims' Hall with a hammer-beam roof of the 1290s – the oldest so far identified.

Chamber Court – survives, despite later alterations and additions. The long ranges on College Street facing the outside world do not really do the architecture of the college justice, and G.S. Repton's headmaster's house is Hammer House of Horror Gothic with few redeeming features. The gateway itself, with its magnificent vaulting, hints at better things to come within. A second gateway, the Middle Gate, leads through into the original heart of the college – the Chamber Court, around which were the boys' lodgings. On the south side of the court is the first floor hall (with the original school room beneath), restored in 1817 by William Garbett. Next to it is the chapel, notable more for its furnishings than its architecture – and particularly for its late fourteenth-century stalls and misericords. The tower was restored by Butterfield in 1862–3 – or, more accurately, was rebuilt by him using as much salvaged material as possible.

To the south, though oddly aligned in relation to the two courts, are the cloisters. Their original character was altered when the Fromond chantry chapel was built in the grassed central area – the 'garth' – shortly after 1420. It was constructed of stone from the Isle of Wight and intended to help save the soul of its benefactor. Since these medieval ranges were built the college has continued to grow and now has a very large collection of buildings of many dates within the grounds – which are, of course, private but can be viewed by the public on occasion. Of these the most important is School, just west of the cloister, built of brick in 1687 at a cost of £2,600 and, as with so many prestigious buildings of this period, attributed wrongly or hopefully to Sir Christopher Wren.

Many new buildings were built around the turn of the present century, both within the main part of the college or in the adjacent city suburb that is now largely given over to it. Few call for much attention, apart from the pompous Commoner Gate built by Frank Loughborough Pearson to honour the college's dead in the South African wars. Far better is the new cloister built in the early 1920s to honour those who fell in the Great War; the architect was Sir Herbert Baker. Elsewhere in this part of the city are the boarding houses used by the 'commoners' attending the college. Most of these are large Victorian houses of little aesthetic merit. One building of interest outside the main grounds is the curious Music Room in

Romans Road, built in 1904 by Edward Schroder Prior, and unlike the Arts and Crafts style he sometimes dabbled in.

Other schools include the Pilgrims' School by the cathedral, a preparatory school for cathedral choristers founded in 1931. The main building is a large brick house built in the 1680s for a warden of Winchester College, but more importantly the buildings also include the medieval Pilgrims' Hall. This gets its name from the tradition that it housed pilgrims visiting the shrine of St Swithun. Architecturally it is important in having one of the earliest examples of a hammer-beam roof known in Britain. Until recently this has been dated to the early fourteenth century, but some of the timbers have been subjected to a new technique called dendrochronology – literally tree ring sampling in which the rings are counted and compared with accurately dated examples. This work has suggested that the Pilgrims' Hall was built in the 1290s – a

94 This Victorian wall-mounted post box with its original enamelled sign is still used; it is in Kingsgate Street.

century before the magnificent hammer-beam roof of Westminster Hall.

One of the more famous architects of eighteenth-century England was Sir John Soane, and few realize that he designed a building in Winchester. It still survives, but frankly is not very exciting. In 1795 Soane designed a school hall for a Reverend Richards, built near to Hyde Abbey House. It is a very plain brick structure with arched windows set in arched recesses.

Houses

Despite its antiquity, and despite the number of its historic buildings, there are very few tangible remains of medieval domestic life in Winchester. The house in the Middle Ages revolved around the one principal room – the hall. Life then was far more communal, and in the larger houses the owners and servants lived and ate together. Generally, the owners would have their own private quarters at one end, the high end, of the hall, and the store rooms – the services – would be at the opposite, or low end. The permutations on the way these basic elements in the medieval house were arranged were endless. Henry III's great hall at the castle is simply an exceptionally grand version of what was a common feature of medieval life. In complete contrast, archaeologists working in Lower Brook Street have recently uncovered a row of tiny cottages dating to around 1300. Each single 'cell' was divided into two – the 'hall' and a minuscule bed closet.

The surviving medieval houses have mainly been altered so much over the years that it is difficult to see exactly how they would once have been arranged. The lodgings built in the 1440s at the hospital of St Cross, on the other hand, are comparatively little altered. These were exceptional, not just because of their background but also because of the quality of the accommodation provided. Each lodging had its small hall, a bedchamber and a small service room. Astonishingly, for the time, each also had its own garderobe – or latrine – a facility that would not be even remotely universal until the end of the nineteenth century.

In 1840 one writer said of Winchester that its 'houses are in general substantial and well built, and many of them possess an appearance of great antiquity'. Most of those older buildings date to the sixteenth and seventeenth centuries, by which time the general layout of the private house had become little

different from those of our own time. The communal medieval way had gradually fallen out of favour and was replaced with more private living. In the houses this was reflected by a move away from just a handful of rooms that could be used for many different things to those that had specific purposes – the parlour, the withdrawing room, the bedchamber, the closet and so forth. The hall became little more than a ceremonial lobby – as it still is today.

The main changes to houses since the end of the medieval period have been associated with changes in architectural fashions rather than with changes in the way of life. Symmetry and proportion, lessons learnt – though not always well – from the Renaissance, had already become infused into at least some of Winchester's houses by the early seventeenth century. As in other towns, this, coupled with the replacement of timber framing with brick, would change the character of houses

96 Winchester has no intact private domestic medieval halls left – but the great halls that served both the college and the hospital of St Cross followed the same general pattern and were used for much the same purpose. The mid-fifteenth-century open hall of St Cross is particularly impressive, seen here looking towards the gallery over the screen's passage.

97 One of the best-known landmarks of Winchester is the Old Rectory in Chesil Street, dated to 1459. It is probably just a little later, but is nevertheless a fine late medieval, timber-framed building. It was first restored in 1892–3, a time when there was renewed interest in our architectural heritage. Render was stripped away and the encroachment under the jetty demolished. It was restored for a second time in 1960.

98 Abbot's Barton, in Chaundler Road, Hyde, is a much altered 'hall-house' of the late fifteenth or early sixteenth century. Timber-framed, now mainly with brick nogging infill, it retains its late medieval character to the rear despite the Victorian tile-hanging. The other side, the garden front, was rebuilt around 1700.

99 The Tudor House in St John Street, most of which dates to the sixteenth century, is unusual in having a ground floor built half of stone and half of timber framing. The plinth is of ashlar and flint chequers, the lower part of the ground floor being of lesser quality work. It may have seemed more sensible to have built the entire ground floor of stone and then added the jettied upper portion.

100 The sixteenth-century Eclipse was still covered with render until the 1920s when it was restored. For many years it served as the rectory of St Lawrence's. The present front is little more than a spirited copy of the jettied original. Its name, given to it in 1925, was chosen because of the nearby Sun Inn, now a shop.

towards the latter part of that century. The Restoration of 1660 had a dramatic effect on the houses being built in Winchester. There was a need to rebuild, because of the damage wreaked during the Civil War and Commonwealth. At first the new houses, such as those of Dome Alley already referred to, were little different from those that had gone before. Then the beginning of the new palace for Charles II changed things.

The King's House was Sir Christopher Wren's one and only chance to build on a scale where money and size were no object. Time, however, was, for by the time work started in 1683 Charles was fifty-three – and in a great hurry to see it finished. In essence, Wren's building consisted of a main block, with a central portico, and flanking wings around three sides of a huge courtyard. When Charles died early in 1685, nearly £45,000 had been spent, and the basic carcass and the roof were complete. After James halted the work the huge

102 Symonds Street is named after Peter Symonds who founded an almshouse, Christ's Hospital, at its southern end in 1607. Built of brick, laid in English bond, the buildings were to care for an odd mix of people – six old men, one matron and four boys. The foundation was also to fund one scholar at Oxford and Cambridge universities. The buildings were restored and slightly altered in the last century.

103 Close studding is now rare in Winchester and it is not known if it was ever common. This example is 17 Little Minster Street, originally of two storeys – the first floor being jettied. In later years the jetty was underbuilt and an extra floor added. No doubt it was rendered at the same time.

104 After the Restoration, new houses were needed in the Close to replace those wrecked during the previous two decades of war and virtual anarchy. Dome Alley, built in 1661, consists of two large semi-detached houses, one on either side of the street. Built of brick, in English bond, the cross-mullioned windows are of stone and there are decorative brick cornices in the gables, and elaborate leadwork in the gutters and downpipes. This is the north side, and in the far house, Izaak Walton, author of *The Compleat Angler*, died in 1683; it was his son-in-law's home.

105 Rosemary Close has a lovely name and this could be mistaken for a tranquil village scene. In fact, this terrace, once of six very small cottages, stands just on the opposite bank of the Itchen to the city centre and dates to the seventeenth century. Much rebuilt, there are now just two cottages.

106 Avebury House in St Peter's Street is thought to have been built in 1690. It is five bays wide (the wings are later) and two storeys high, with attics lit by dormer gables in the overhanging roof. Built of hand-made red brick, it sits on a flint plinth.

107 Nos 1 – 2 St Swithin Street, just outside the Close but inside the city wall, were remodelled in the late seventeenth century yet retain stone gabled wings to the rear. Perhaps it may have been one house originally. The downpipes and plate-glass windows of the left-hand house do not do the pair any aesthetic favours.

unfinished shell 'a noble Palace, sufficient . . . for a summer residence for the whole Court' was home to two watchmen and a dog. Later a temporary prison, George III briefly considered finishing it as a palace but in 1796 work began on converting it into barracks. Nearly a century later, in 1894, the King's House was badly damaged by fire and demolished. New barracks were built on the site, designed by E. Ingress Bell and using parts of the original portico.

In 1684, the year after work on the King's House had started in the royal castle, footings were laid at the opposite side of the city in the bishop's castle, Wolvesey, for a second new palace – this time for the prelate. Much of this survives and, although it is faced with ashlar, the general style was very similar, though clearly not as extravagant, as Wren's work for the king. As with so many buildings of this period, he is claimed to be its architect. These two palaces were built for wealthy men, but

109 No. 5 Kingsgate Street was probably built at the very start of the eighteenth century in red brick decorated with blue headers to form a chequer pattern. The raised brick window surrounds are peculiar, and it looks as though the house was cut off at the right-hand side when the next-door building was put up.

110 At the south end of St Thomas's Street – otherwise lined by grand Georgian town houses of the wealthy – is this humble brick terrace dated 1695. It was restored in the nineteenth century.

other houses a little lower down the social scale could still adopt elements of their design. Among the larger examples are two close to each other and not far from the bishop's palace – the Pilgrims' School, probably of the 1680s, and No. 1 the Close, built in 1699. Other houses in the city itself include a pair on St Peter's Street. Avebury House was probably built in the 1690s, but No. 4 is earlier. Possibly smaller now than it once was, it is another house claimed to be by Wren – for Charles II's favourite mistress, Louise de Querouaille, Duchess of Portsmouth.

Throughout the eighteenth century the well-known Georgian town house became well established in Winchester – as, indeed, they did throughout England. Better in mellow red brick, it is a style both homely and grand, and one that seems to fit so perfectly into any townscape. Kingsgate Street is particularly satisfying – and much of Southgate Street would be too were it not for the traffic.

111 Unfortunately disused and empty at the moment, 28 Jewry Street is a good example of an early eighteenth-century town house of two storeys and six bays. It is of the 'double-pile' type – note the two parallel gabled roofs – but there is a possibility that the two 'piles' were built at separate times, judging from the different cornice of the rear part to the left.

112 The hopper heads on top of the rainwater pipes of the Southgate Hotel on Southgate Street bear the date 1715. It is a fine late Queen Anne three-storey house of five bays with a good brick-decorated central bay and a segmented pediment over the first-floor window.

113 23 St Peter's Street, now called Trussell House, has a solid and symmetrical mid-eighteenth-century front with the large canted bays then becoming fashionable flanking the central front door. The difference in the brickwork of the front and the side may suggest this has been added to a slightly earlier building.

114 No 70 Kingsgate Street retains its enchanting bowed Georgian shop windows on the ground floor and a typical Winchester bow oriel above the central doorway. The brick bond is Flemish – each course being of alternating 'stretchers' and 'headers'.

115 The stuccoed front of No 57 High Street is one of the most attractive in the city. Although probably mid–late eighteenth century in date, its present appearance dates from the early nineteenth century – possibly from when the *Hampshire Chronicle* took over the building in 1813.

Another Georgian development was the high-class terrace. Terraces were by no means invented in the eighteenth century – they had been built since medieval times. In the eighteenth century they became respectable. Winchester has only a few Georgian terraces of note – such as those at the north end of St Peter's Street, probably built early in the nineteenth century. Most of the grand terraces in the city are early to mid-Victorian, ranging from the sinuous stuccoed lines of 1–19 Eastgate Street to the High Victorian Gothic of houses lining the south side of City Road. By and large, the terrace stopped being fashionable from the middle of the century onwards in places like Winchester. The middle classes tended to want the ubiquitous semi-detached house – suitably refined and often extremely large. The terrace became the cheapest form of housing development as the city grew, and terraces and semi-detached artisan houses were built in great numbers. Many

116 Robert Adam, the architect, had a tremendous effect on English architecture by popularizing a more gentle, neoclassical style of decoration. Tens of thousands of houses were influenced by him, and this is just one such example, 34 Colebrook Street, probably built towards the end of the eighteenth century. It has 'shell' tops to the tripartite ground floor windows and a delicate fanlight above the door.

117 Serle's House, on Southgate Street, is a large early Georgian town house with a hint of the then-outmoded Baroque in its detailing and decoration. Its distinctive canted full-height bay centrepiece is most unusual but, architecturally, most effective. It is now the museum of the Hampshire Regiment.

118 In the once spacious gardens of Abbey House, now a public park, this Tuscan temple was built by William Pescod in about 1750 to hide the Abbey Mill behind it. The temple was once larger.

119 Clifton Terrace, just west of the city centre, was clearly influenced by the grand terraces still being built in the early nineteenth century in fashionable towns such as Bath and Cheltenham. Built of the London stock brick, the ground floor is stuccoed, and the whole composition is 'articulated' by the use of pilasters. The 'hearts and honeysuckle' motif on the cast-iron balconies was very popular in the 1820s and '30s.

120 Apart from a little bit of neo-Tudor decoration, the lodge to the Roman Catholic cemetery on the Romsey Road is small, neat and plain. It was built in 1829.

121 The stuccoed curves of 1 – 19 Eastgate Street are a sheer delight – a wonderful piece of street theatre built as a speculative venture early in the nineteenth century.

122 St Giles's House on St Giles's Hill was originally called Coytbury and was designed in the late nineteenth century by Thomas Stopher the Younger, one time mayor of the city. Its situation is superb, with fine views over Winchester.

123 Joyously eccentric, this balconied house on West Hill must date to the mid-nineteenth century. It was built for someone who knew what they wanted – and didn't care about what anyone else thought.

124 One of Bishop Morley's legacies to Winchester was Morley College, originally built as the College of Matrons – for the widows of the clergy – in 1672. Built in brick on the north side of the Close, in style it was similar to his new bishop's palace nearby. In 1880 John Colson rebuilt the college in a similar though more mechanical style.

were built by speculators building very cheaply and not always that well. Winchester did have its own charitable organization trying to improve the housing of the poor – the Winchester Cottage Improvement Society; they built Culverwell Gardens off Culver Road in 1894.

In the twentieth century, Winchester's houses have developed no differently from any other town or city across England – much to the detriment of its local character. The quality of the houses has improved – but the universal pale-brick English semi lacks charm no matter how many different varieties of instant 'heritage' are tacked on to it. Winchester has even had to suffer the still less charming high-rise flats – but at least they have been kept at a distance from the city centre.

125 The Tudor Gothick street frontage of Abbey House, facing the Broadway, dates to the early nineteenth century. Its tower-flanked façade was tacked on to William Pescod's mid-eighteenth-century house. The garden front was unaltered, giving the house a distinct split personality. The site was once part of the Saxon Nunneminster – hence its name.

126 The origins of the motifs decorating this mid-Victorian terraced house – Westbury – in the City Road are closer to home. In this case there is a generous helping of Italianate detail to confuse matters.

127 No 50 Christchurch Road is a big house of yellow brick with red brick dressings probably dating to the 1880s. Perhaps a little austere, it is a good example of the type of house thought necessary for the wealthy late Victorian.

Industrial Buildings

Perhaps not surprisingly, Winchester is not noted for its industrial heritage, even though it has a very long industrial tradition. Indeed, it is one of the oldest in England, for the Romans set up a state-sponsored weaving mill there. The city that was once one of the major textile towns of England – way back in the twelfth century – has been a quiet market town for centuries. A guide book in the first half of the nineteenth century was quite blunt – 'the trade of Winchester is very unimportant'. By this time there was a little carding of wool being carried out, but a silk manufacturing operation that had recently been started failed miserably and closed within a few years.

The main natural advantage Winchester had in the medieval period was the free-flowing Itchen. Centuries before steam power was available, waterwheels turned most of the machinery there was. As well as the river itself, there were several mill-races taken off it to provide additional water courses. A handful of mills survive in the city, but these are all grinding mills. The Abbey Mill and the College Mill are probably the oldest, both seeming to date from the early eighteenth century. The eminently picturesque City Mill by the bridge was rebuilt in 1743–4 and is now owned by the National Trust. A much larger building of 1885 is called Wharf Mill and it stands close to a road called Wharf Hill. The wharf in question was the Blackbridge Wharf, the head of the Itchen Navigation; most of the traffic on the river was coal, incidentally. The mill buildings, which also contained the offices of the

128 The station at Winchester was designed by Sir William Tite, one of the most respected station architects of his day. It was finished in 1839.

129 Winchester, despite its medieval industrial growth, has always retained close links with the local agriculture. Indeed, farms were built on its very outskirts and this former barn in Hyde was part of Abbot's Barton farmstead. It was built in 1799, during the agricultural boom caused by the need for home-grown food in the long-running Napoleonic Wars.

130 Most stables in a city of Winchester's size would be quite humble. This former stable block in St Thomas' Street – Mason's Yard – is thus quite exceptional. Built in the late Georgian period, it served the house on the opposite side of the road, No 9. In 1972 it was converted to its present use.

131 The Wharf Mill, downstream of the City Mill, is a multi-storey brick mill dated 1885. It also contained the offices of the Itchen Navigation. In 1970 it was converted into apartments.

132 Now owned by the National Trust, the tile-hung City Mill on the Itchen belonged, in medieval times, to the Priory of Wherwell. The present building was built in the 1740s, a very pleasant example of vernacular brick and tile hanging.

Navigation, were gutted in 1970 and converted into apartments, with new extensions to the east.

Just outside the site of the North Gate, in Hyde Road, is a large brewery, some of the buildings of which date back to the early nineteenth century. Remains of other industries are scattered and few.

133 The City Bridge, an integral element in one of the city's many set-piece views with the City Mill behind, was rebuilt in 1813.

Further Reading

Local Books

Atkinson, T., *Elizabethan Winchester* (1963)

Beaumont James, T., *Winchester – A Pictorial History* (1993)

Biddle, M. and Clayre, B., *Winchester Castle and the Great Hall* (1983)

Carpenter Turner, B., *Winchester* (1992)

Shurlock, B., *The Winchester Guidebook* (1990)

General Books

Brunskill, R.W., *Timber Building in Britain* (1985)

Brunskill, R.W., *Brick Building in Britain* (1990)

Clifton-Taylor, A., *A Pattern of English Building* (4th edn, 1987)

Cruickshank, D., *A Guide to the Georgian Buildings of Britain and Ireland* (1985)

Harris, R., *Discovering Timber-framed Buildings* (1978)

Pevsner, N., *The Buildings of England* series, in county volumes

Platt, C., *The English Medieval Town* (1976)

Index

(Numbers in bold indicate illustrations)

121